KEEP SLEEPING KEEP MISSING

If Only You Knew

By

MANISH JAITLY

First published in 2020 by

Becomeshakespeare.com
One Point Six Technologies Pvt. Ltd.
Unit - 26, Building A -1, Nr Wadala RTO,
Wadala (East), Mumbai 400037, India
T: +91 8080226699

Cover Designer: Raj Abhishek Rajput

ISBN 978-93-90543-01-4

Disclaimer

The techniques stated in this book have not been examined by any medical body or organisation and are not intended to be a substitute for any medical treatment. The author has stated these techniques in good faith and takes no responsibility for the experiences any reader of this book has by practising them.

Dedicated to
my loving parents

**Late Mr. Binay Narain Sharma
and Mrs. Kamlesh Sharma**

Preface

If you have bought this book, then it is likely

- ➤ You have a routine life that involves
  - getting up in the morning
  - dressing up
  - having breakfast
  - going to work
  - coming back home
  - spending whatever time is left with your family, pets or hobbies
  - going back to sleep
- ➤ From time to time, you go on a vacation with your family and friends.
- ➤ You have just the normal interest in what is happening in the world, and you get most of the inputs from traditional or social media.
- ➤ You obey all laws and regulations.
- ➤ Perhaps once in a while you donate money to charity and volunteer your time for a good cause.

Well, without going into further details, you are the normal good person who believes in 'Live and Let Live'.

Right?

If your answer is 'Yes', then you are a part of the 80% of the world's population that I call the Keep-Sleeping-Keep-Missing-People (KSKMP).

The KSKMP are born, get educated, earn a livelihood (some become billionaires), retire, become old, fall sick and die. Despite their success, fame and achievements, our busy world eventually forgets most of them. These individuals wade through life and are oblivious to much greater realities and possibilities that can enrich not only their lives but also contribute to making the world a better place. The only world the KSKMP see is the material world; they have no reference point to guide them into shifting their identity to something much greater than what they presently imagine.

It is high time the KSKMP see themselves and all life from a higher perspective—this book will encourage and guide them in their endeavours. Many changes are happening on our planet; human society has undergone a drastic change in the last few decades but not without new and often overwhelming challenges. The KSKMP can no longer have a narrow view of life and concern themselves only with their immediate needs and surroundings. It is time for us to look at ourselves, our fellow men and Mother Nature as a unified whole.

We can no longer slice life into chunks flavoured with selfishness and apathy.

This book is not a self-help or a make-you-feel-good book; it will most likely shake some of your existing beliefs and worldview, so please keep an open mind. This book aims at jostling you and giving you a knock on your head so that you get up and stretch, rinse your eyes with water, step into the verandah of your mind, and see reality on a bigger canvas. If you keep sleeping, you will keep missing. The knowledge in the following pages should reach a critical mass of people.

I sincerely hope this book adds value to your life and you find every chapter engaging. Perhaps you are divinely guided to this book because you are now ready for this knowledge. Books are great teachers, and when the student is ready, the teacher arrives.

– Manish Jaitly

Contents

Contents

CHAPTER 1
An Open Mind

In the preface itself, I mentioned the need for an open mind to read this book, so I thought it wise to dedicate this very first chapter to it.

You are an open-minded person if you explore new knowledge and facts without insecurity, fear and preconceived notions. The need to feel secure with knowledge gained in the past is the primary reason that prevents a person from being open-minded. The ego is always seeking security and surety—it stubbornly clings to its existing knowledge and beliefs. Many people straightaway reject anything that does not conform to their existing set of beliefs. Such people do not want to change, even if they ultimately realise the folly of their current belief system and values. We see this most in organised religions, and this is one cause of religious conflicts. Many educated intellectuals are closed-minded and rigid in their beliefs; they are impervious to higher truths.

A closed-minded person looks at anything new through perception filters which act like coloured glasses. If you see the sky through a red glass, the sky appears red; you cannot see the actual sky-blue colour. Perception filters prevent a correct understanding of anything. A child born to communist parents may become an anti-capitalist or anti-democratic adult because it sees everything through a communist lens. Take an honest look at yourself and see how conditioned your mind is; the more conditioned it is, the more perception filters you have and the more distorted view of reality you get.

Let us see some reasons that make people closed-minded:

- **Over deference and respect for elders & ancestors** - Knowledge and beliefs derived from family elders are holy cows and sacred; therefore, they are immune to improvisation and cannot be updated. The ancestral ego also prevents a person from opening their mind to alternate possibilities.

- **Superiority complex** - Many people are proud of their academic or professional qualifications, awards, medals and worldly recognition. They assume that they know everything and respond mechanically with cynicism to anything that does not fit with their existing knowledge base and beliefs. Such people are afraid of being proven wrong as it can damage their reputation and wound their egos.

It is amusing when scientists comment on a newly discovered planet and say that it cannot harbour life because there is no oxygen and water on it. Even astronomers opine that our universe has billions of worlds of seemingly endless variety. Is it not possible that the inhabitants of that planet inhale a gas other than oxygen and drink a liquid different from water? These very scientists, however, say that a vast number of species on Earth await discovery. It is strange to see these people pontificating about other planets when they do not fully understand their own!

- **Religious conditioning** - This is one of the most important reasons many people are closed-minded in matters of spirituality and religion. The actual teachings of prophets have been vastly distorted; religions are now mainly about rituals, dogmas, doctrines and belief systems. These serve as control mechanisms and means of indoctrination, and make many people believe that their religion is the only true religion and the only path to salvation. This fanatical mindset has led to millions of people killed in the name of God. A person conditioned with the beliefs of their religion finds it challenging to open up to higher spiritual truths.

- **Affiliations** - Members of a political party feel compelled not to look beyond their party's ideology. A communist may never explore and appreciate other forms of government and irrationally find faults in them. Observe how opposition parties in a democratic country behave; even if the government does the right thing, they criticise it just because they are in the opposition. One can also have an affiliation with a particular philosophy or ism such as atheism and agnosticism. If you are an atheist or an agnostic, you have already concluded that higher realities do not exist and are likely a closed-minded person.

- **Idolatry** - In the last few decades, we have seen a growing practice of idolatry and hero-worship of public figures. There is nothing wrong in admiring a person, but admiration should never turn to blind worship. Public figures such as celebrities, business leaders and politicians often say things based on half-baked knowledge, personal agendas and a desire for publicity. Frequently, their fans and followers blindly believe their every word. In their eyes, their idols can do no wrong—this is again closed-mindedness that often has unhealthy consequences.

- **Psychological issues** - A person with low self-esteem is likely to be more closed-minded than a person with high self-esteem. Low self-esteem rarely gives the courage to explore new knowledge and go against the tide. The dominant beliefs of society, culture and powerful people easily influence a person with low self-esteem. Also, some people have a reflex-action like response in opposing anything new that comes to their attention. Often, they themselves do not know why they resist new knowledge and not look beyond their mental box.

- **Over rationalism** - In every society, some rationalists expose false gurus and debunk superstitions, and in doing so, they genuinely do a commendable service to society. However, people of rational temperament often become overly rational. They refuse to believe that there are worlds beyond the material universe. Many rationalists are habitually sceptical of anything which the five senses cannot detect. Despite knowing that the human senses have a limited range, they still cannot fully internalise this fact.

- **Economic status** - Sections of society with high poverty and illiteracy are usually closed-minded, especially in matters of religion. Mostly, they are highly superstitious and ritualistic. Lack of education does not provide them any frame of reference for higher knowledge.

We define fanaticism mainly in the religious context, but we should realise that every closed-minded person is a fanatic. Just as a religious fanatic defends their religious beliefs, a political fanatic defends their political beliefs. Though the need for security is the prime reason for closed-mindedness, sometimes even laziness can be a reason. Some people know that their knowledge and beliefs are not correct, yet they stick to them. They are too lazy to explore, so convince themselves of the infallibility of their beliefs and worldview.

CHAPTER 2
A Bigger Picture

In the beginning, there was only the Creator; there was no form but only darkness. This Creator is the real God and is pure consciousness or pure spirit. The Creator felt lonely and wanted to enjoy itself, evolve and expand; it decided to create spheres and send beings to inhabit those spheres. The Creator also decided that every sphere would have the basic structures needed for life; the beings would create the remaining structures as a part of their learning process. The Creator expected that the beings would ultimately remember that they were *His* extensions (miniature versions). After having learnt their lessons, they would join Him in the spiritual realm. Subsequently, the entire sphere would ascend back to the Creator. This way, the Creator would also get enriched with the experiences brought by the beings from their respective spheres.

There are seven spheres; within every sphere, there are multiple realms; each realm has several sub-realms. Six spheres have ascended and are now a part of the spiritual realms. The material universe where the Earth resides is in the seventh sphere and has four realms: etheric, mental, emotional and physical. The seventh sphere does not as yet have enough light of the Creator, so is unascended. After the seventh sphere ascends, the eighth will get created—this is how Creation happens. The spheres interact with each other; the seventh sphere cannot exist without the first six. Very often, the ideas behind brilliant inventions, discoveries, and works of art have been implanted into deserving humans by advanced beings in the other spheres. Humans scarcely know to what extent they receive assistance from the higher spheres.

All Creation is made from the primordial energy or light of the Creator. This energy is known as the Universal-Light-Substance (also called 'Mother Light'). The Creator's energy becomes denser with every succeeding sphere and also with every succeeding realm within a sphere. The thicker the energy, the denser and lesser malleable matter in that sphere or realm is. Since the Earth is in the physical realm of the lowest sphere, matter here is dense, making manifestation difficult. In higher realms, if you imagine an apple in your hand, it manifests immediately. On Earth, this is not possible for most people, unless they develop their mental powers to a large degree. You must have understood by now that the denser the matter is, the more challenging life becomes for the beings in that sphere. No wonder life for most people on our planet is such a challenge and a struggle. However, as one expands their consciousness, they will realise that life need not be a struggle at all.

Humankind must awaken to the fact that there are no physical boundaries either between spheres or between realms within a sphere. It is the same energy of the Creator that is vibrating at different rates throughout Creation, and in every last object, even a pencil. Energy vibrating at a particular rate makes up a block of ice. When the ice melts into water, the same energy now vibrates at a different rate and gives the appearance of a liquid called 'water'. When the water is heated, that same energy takes on a different rate of vibration and becomes steam. Therefore, there is nothing truly solid in Creation; what appears solid is a mass of electrons that are all moving at terrific speeds. In other words, matter is nothing but condensed energy, and this is precisely what the brilliant scientist Albert Einstein proved with this theory of relativity. His discovery gave birth to Quantum Physics which challenged Newtonian Physics. It is unfortunate that humanity, till now, has not fully used Einstein's marvellous discovery constructively.

Since the Fall of Man, humanity has been put to sleep by the fallen beings and the sinister force. The slumber is so deep that humans have completely lost sight of the vast and much higher realities that are all around us and beckoning us to explore them. It is perfectly possible for every human being to access higher realms and spheres by raising their consciousness; spiritual growth increases the vibratory rate of the body's electrons. At the sub-atomic level everything in Creation is interconnected.

---

1) The 'Fall of Man', 'fallen beings' and the 'sinister force' have been explained later in the book.

2) It's a good idea to learn about near-death experiences (NDE) on the Internet. Thousands of people from all over the world have journeyed into higher realms and have come back to relate amazing experiences.

CHAPTER 3
Your Conscious-Self

Have you ever contemplated the word 'conscious'? To most people, this word means 'being awake' in the sense that 'the patient has regained consciousness'. If humankind truly understood and honoured the word 'consciousness', this planet would have been far more beautiful than it is today. The fact is, we humans have taken consciousness totally for granted. Note that most of the time, we are not even aware of the air that we breathe because it is all around us and also inside us— this is the case also with consciousness. It is so much a part of us that, most of the time, we are not even aware of what it means to be conscious.

Have you ever observed that when someone is talking to you, but your mind is preoccupied with thoughts, you are not fully conscious? You are not even aware that your thoughts have diverted you and are preventing you from hearing what the other person is saying. In this state of mind, you are just partially conscious. Please don't feel guilty as this is the state of mind of most people for almost 95% of the total waking hours of their lives.

You must have realised by now that the freer your mind is of thoughts, the greater the opportunity for you to be more conscious of your surroundings. I use the word 'opportunity' because merely having a silent mind is not enough to become conscious. If you are in an uninterested or lazy frame of mind, then despite being in a thought-free state, you are still not fully conscious of your surroundings. You are only partially conscious because a part of your mind is uninterested and sleeping. An unconscious person has no thoughts but is not conscious either. Take note that when you are fully alert and focused on a task, such as working on your laptop or reading a book, *you are conscious of that activity*.

Try this simple exercise—you can do this as often as you can.

Make sure you are alone and undisturbed; sit comfortably anywhere. Now close your eyes and concentrate on your body. Focus first on the skin of your body, then go deeper towards the muscles, then your bones and organs. Beneath the structure of your skin, muscles, bones and organs, there is a rejuvenating silence. Now focus on this silence in all parts of your body for about ten minutes. Try to make your focus deeper but do not stress yourself or focus too hard. You need to be relaxed. You will now feel a wholeness; this is a glimpse of your Conscious-Self, which is your true self. The silence of your Conscious-Self is also nothingness or emptiness because it is free of thoughts and human concepts such as dogmas, opinions and beliefs. This emptiness is actually the fullness of the Creator, the real God. The Conscious-Self is a small portion of a Being who is majestic beyond human imagination, and you will know about this being in a later chapter. So stay tuned.

Your Conscious-Self is the pure-consciousness part of you and gives you the ability to respond, remember and change. As you attune to your Conscious-Self, you will realise you are much more than just your human self. Living through your Conscious-Self is the only correct way to live. By expanding your Conscious-Self, you can transform your identity into something more significant. Ideally, your life's experiences, both good and bad, should expand your Conscious-Self and make you something more. Sadly, this does not happen for most people, so they do not achieve their true potential.

Spend at least ten minutes every day focusing on your inner silence. You dishonour yourself when you ignore your true self.

We will revisit the Conscious-Self in the next chapter.

---

1) Please remember the terms 'Conscious-Self', 'Selves' and 'Unconscious-Self' as I use them frequently in the book. The last two terms are explained in the next chapter.

2) As you proceed further in the book, you will learn that a human being is much more than a physical body and personality. In some places (not in this chapter), I have used the term 'lifestream' to indicate the total energy that descends into the material universe as a human being. The human that embodies on Earth comprises just a small portion of this total energy. Besides 'lifestream', I have used the terms 'people', 'human beings', 'person' also in places where I deemed appropriate.

CHAPTER 4
Your Unconscious-Self

Now that you know what your Conscious-Self is, it is time to understand what your Unconscious-Self is. Luckily for this, you need not do any exercise. Like most people, you are in this state for almost 95% of your waking hours.

When you look at a person, you see only the physical body and assume that there is only that person, but it is not so. Within every person, there are multiple persons and often thousands of them. For simplicity, I will substitute the term 'multiple persons' with 'Selves'. If you observe yourself, you will find many Selves within your being: kind-hearted Self; hard-working Self; jealous Self; insecure Self; Self addicted to Cricket or Baseball; hot-tempered Self and a Self that fanatically identifies itself with your religion, nationality and political beliefs. There are many more types of Selves, and I cannot mention all here.

The Selves within you are always active, restless, running riot and intermingling with each other to create new Selves. The ceaseless chatter in our minds is the voice of the Selves. If you contemplate deeply, you will realise that it is these Selves inside you that are living your life. By contrast, your Conscious-Self, which is your real Self, has receded into the background. These thousands of Selves within you form the Unconscious-Self. Most people, on rare occasions, get a glimpse of their Conscious-Self. Their Selves control almost 95% of their waking lives.

Your Conscious-Self is like a deep calm ocean, and your many Selves are like flotsam on this ocean. People who spend most of their lives living at the level of the debris are spiritually dead and live like robots. They rarely act but only react and are enslaved by their five senses. The Unconscious-Self always reacts, but what does it mean to react to a situation? You react whenever you mechanically behave in the same way as you did in an earlier similar situation. Therefore, there is nothing original about your response. You have not evolved by gaining any new frame of reference; you continue to look at every new situation through old glasses. Your response is like a broken gramophone record that keeps playing the same tune over and over again. We see this in short-tempered people who lose their temper often for no reason. Losing temper becomes a habit with them and they explode without knowing why. Think over this—do you mostly respond swiftly to a situation without a second thought and later regret it? You must realise that your reactions are like reflex actions, and whenever you react, you are not fully conscious. Most people spend their entire lives reacting to various events in their lives.

What does it mean to act? You act when you respond from the stillness, alertness and depth of your Conscious-Self. It is possible that the situation merits a response similar to the one you gave in an earlier comparable situation. Nevertheless, now you respond with full awareness and not like a robot. When you act, you are authentic, and your actions are original and pertinent to the situation. When you respond from your Conscious-Self, the Selves within you cannot mislead you. They cannot fool you into taking a shortcut by showing old images of how you or someone else responded to a similar situation earlier.

We see in many horror movies—evil spirits as frightening, vapour like formations with human shapes and how they float about screaming. The Selves within you are like these spirits that are always restless within you and at the slightest opportunity, emerge from you, throw a lasso around your neck and drag you wherever they want. Want examples? Have you ever: Purchased something expensive, but of no proper use, only to boost your ego? Reacted at someone angrily only to realise that it was you who was at fault? Disliked someone just because they did not agree with you on something? Sabotaged someone's career out of fear or insecurity? There are endless examples, and if you honestly reflect on your life, you will remember many instances where your Selves controlled you, misled you and caused you much trouble.

It is not incorrect to compare Selves with spirits because Selves are also energetic formations like spirits. Nonetheless, every person after their death can see their Selves. The spiritual teachers in the higher realms show the Selves to the deceased individual. Some of the Selves are of grotesque appearance—somewhat similar to those emerging from the evil cyborg in the movie 'Terminator 2: Judgment Day'.

Too many rigid Selves can stifle a person's creativity; many insecure Selves can lead to depression. In rare cases, several Selves out of all the Selves can conglomerate to form a separate personality—over one such personality results in a Multiple Personality Disorder. There are 'good' and 'bad' Selves and later on in the book you will learn why your 'good' Selves do nothing to contribute to your spiritual awakening.

Presence, Personality and Relationships

Now that you know about the Conscious-Self and the Unconscious-Self, it would be instructive to know the difference between 'presence' and 'personality'. The Unconscious-Self interacts with the world through a framework called 'personality'. Personality is mostly unconscious because of the many Selves that drive it. As you grow spiritually, your personality will loosen its grip on you. You will act more from your Conscious-Self which is silent and alert. When you are in your Conscious-Self, you are in the Now; you are a presence. When you are a presence, you are authentic.

In many relationships, it is the personalities that mostly interact with each other, not the Conscious-Selves; such relationships often fail. People in personality-based relationships are often driven by the desire to seek together sensuous pleasures: movies, shopping, dining, travelling and partying, to name a few. We see this often in marriages where some pleasure-seeking Selves of one partner interact and feel comfortable with similar Selves of the other partner. After a while, the other hitherto unknown Selves of both partners emerge and often clash with each other, resulting in the relationship's breakdown. This phenomenon happens in all relationships, not just marriages. Take another example of a group of college friends who hang out together solely because they like to watch movies, go trekking and have fun. Again, mostly in such cases, these 'friendships' do not last long because there is no depth in them.

If you truly love someone, you will miss their presence much more than their personality when they are not around. The more the partners are in touch with their Conscious-Selves, the deeper will be the relationship. Let us see this from another angle now. Why do you spend time with your family members, friends and pets? It is because you love them. Stretching this a little further, it means that if you are generally averse to spending time alone with yourself, you do not love yourself. Furthermore, if you do not love yourself, can you love others? Probe yourself to see if your love for someone is just a fondness for some of their personality traits. Many relationships are mostly personality-based and are on rocky ground.

Whether you want to relate authentically to others or with yourself, you must learn to attune to your Conscious-Self. It is important to spend time alone without any distractions, such as people and gadgets. Focus and dwell upon the silence within your body as often as you can.

CHAPTER 5
Your Seven Bodies

A human being is much, much more than a physical body. Every human being has six other bodies besides the physical. It is most tragic that humankind has forgotten about these bodies and has focused only on the physical body. The physical body is the densest part of an individual's total lifestream energy matrix and can function only because of the six other bodies. When the physical vehicle usurps all attention, there is very little room left to understand higher realities and laws. Ignorance of higher truths of life have resulted in a planet full of discord, destruction and struggle.

The following are the bodies that make up a human being:

- **Electronic Body (I-AM-Presence)** - Every human being has a divine body, also known as the I-AM-Presence that lives in the spiritual realm. This heavenly body is made up of pure electrons of God and vibrates at a much higher rate than the human eye can see. The I-AM-Presence sends a stream of electrons that enters the physical body and gets anchored in the heart as the threefold unfed flame. The moment this streamflow of electrons stops, death happens. Every human being's electrons have a distinctive pattern and design—this makes every person a truly unique individual. The unique electronic pattern enables the universe to track every individual's karma. Your electronic body is an individualised being with whom you can speak, and who hears your every call and prayer. It is your true identity in its full glory and your personal God.

The I-AM-Presence is the source of all energy, all life and everything of that human. The more a person is in tune with their I-AM-Presence, the more everything in all areas of their life happens in alignment with the divine will of God. The I-AM-Presence being the individualised presence of God, is perfect and is continuously trying to manifest perfection in the person's life provided they maintain harmony in emotions and feelings. The divine energy that the I-AM-Presence sends to the physical body is pure. Nevertheless, in most people, as soon as this spiritual energy enters the physical body, it gets contaminated with impure feelings of anger, hatred, condemnation, jealousy and so forth. Therefore, the pristine radiation cannot manifest perfection and fulfilment of the divine plan in the person's life. It is essential to avoid negativity and maintain harmony in your emotions and feelings to enable your I-AM-Presence to do its work in your life. Tibetan Buddhists and Hindus call the I-AM-Presence 'Dharmakaya' & 'Aham Brahmasmi' respectively.

- **Causal Body** - Have you ever felt in a situation that you had an inner sense of knowing the right thing to do? It was your causal body prompting you; your perception filters had no part in this. Note, how you learn about parenthood by seeing your child's life from the outside. Likewise, your I-AM-Presence learns by observing your life from the outside. Your I-AM-Presence stores all the wisdom it gains from your experiences in all embodiments, in your causal body. The causal body is a giant repository of all the good collected in every single embodiment—no experience is wasted. It requires emotional harmony to tap into this reservoir of wisdom when the situation demands. The size of the causal body is directly proportional to the amount of constructively qualified energy it stores. The causal body is depicted as the seven spheres of different colours around the electronic body.

- **Christ-Self (Higher Mental Body)** - The I-AM-Presence does not work directly with the human (Conscious-Self encased in a physical body) but does so through the Christ-Self. The Christ-Self lies between the I-AM-Presence and the physical body and acts as an intermediary between these two bodies. It functions as a step-down transformer and has a lower vibratory action than the electronic body. However, in action, it is one with the I-AM-Presence and talks with it about your prayers and needs. The Christ-Self just like the I-AM-Presence is eternally beautiful, youthful and perfect; it is the perfect directing intelligence in you. If you surrender to it and heed its guidance that comes as a feeling in the heart or as intuition, it will ensure that you take the best recourse in any situation in life. Your Christ-Self, just as your I-AM-Presence, wants perfection in your life and being a silent watcher is aware of your every thought, action, feeling and motive. It is the teacher and comforter that is attached to your life stream to help you live on a dark planet, such as the Earth. It is your conscience that alerts you when you are about to do something that is not in your highest interest. The Christ-Self is waiting every moment to assist you, but you must consistently endeavour to attune yourself to it and seek its guidance.

The Christ-Self is the individualised Universal Christ Consciousness which is the all-knowing intelligence of God present in every particle of Creation. Anyone who achieves union with their Christ-Self becomes a 'Christ'. Therefore, it is an enormous mistake to refer to the word 'Christ' only in the context of Christianity. Christ Consciousness is a state of consciousness that every individual, irrespective of their religion, must endeavour to achieve.

- **Etheric Body** - The etheric body, also called 'Soul', is the counterpart of the physical body and consists of fine substance from the etheric realm. This body contains the memories and records of all experiences an individual collects during its thousands of embodiments on Earth. Your collected memories, karma and records that lie in your etheric body determine how you see yourself. Do you see yourself as a kind-hearted person, an ambitious person, a puny human who is a victim of circumstances or a child of God? The etheric vehicle stores both good and bad karma, and pleasant and unpleasant memories; it is necessary to purify this body to avoid tribulations and diseases. Often, a person does not achieve success in life despite being talented and hard-working. They fail because of too many impurities (memories and records of past failures and disappointments) in their etheric body.

- **Mental Body** - The physical body is just a container and is incapable of generating thought; it is through the mental body that a person thinks, ideates or imagines. The substance of the mental realm creates the mental body. The purpose of the mental body is to receive divine ideas from the I-AM-Presence and carry out those divine ideas in the physical world through the physical body.

The mental body potentially has tremendous power, but this power gets curtailed by the identity, shaped by the etheric body, of the person. If a person identifies themselves as a poor person, their thoughts will mostly be about limitations and scarcity. It will take a significant effort to think thoughts about prosperity.

- **Emotional Body** - Just as the physical body cannot generate thoughts, it cannot create emotions either. Emotions and feelings emerge from the emotional body. This body is larger than the three other lower bodies and comprises the substance of the emotional realm. The real purpose of the emotional body is to radiate love, peace, joy and compassion. Still, humankind stubbornly persists in misusing this body to diffuse hatred, anger, violence, fear and condemnation. Negative emotions accumulating in the emotional body lead to illnesses, diseases, premature ageing and misfortunes. The emotional body mainly comprises the water element; thus, the Earth, comprising 75% water, is immensely harmed by the karmic turmoil that humans experience through their emotional bodies.

Turbulent emotions bury the Conscious-Self, so it is necessary to calm them. If most of the humankind harmonise their emotions, our planet will be released from tremendous stress and become more beautiful.

- **Physical Body** - This body needs no introduction because every human being is familiar with it. Most people are not even aware of the other bodies at all! The physical body is the flesh-vehicle that the I-AM-Presence uses to gain experiences in the physical realm. Impairments in the physical body, such as illness, disease and faster ageing, manifest due to the misuse of the etheric, mental and emotional bodies. The physical body, like the three other lower bodies, is impacted by the emotions and thoughts of other people. This body is the anchor of the I-AM-Presence in the physical realm.

The Being that You Are

Your I-AM-Presence, as you have already seen, is the greater part of you. It wanted to experience the physical plane, and bring beauty and perfection in your life. Thus, it sent a small portion of itself (your Conscious-Self) into the physical realm. The Conscious-Self is made of spiritual energies and could not have sustained itself on Earth because of the dense matter and vibrations of the planet. Therefore, it created a vehicle for itself; this vehicle is your entire human structure that comprises your four lower bodies: etheric, mental, emotional and physical. These four bodies act as a sea diver's diving suit and enable the Conscious-Self to live on Earth and grow from its experiences.

When the Conscious-Self leaves the I-AM-Presence to embody in the physical realm for the first time, it gets overwhelmed by dense energies and low vibrations of the material world. It forgets its higher identity and loses sight of higher realities. The Conscious-Self now sees only the physical world with all its sufferings and discord. In order to cope with the material world, it creates a self-defence mechanism called 'ego'. The ego creates Selves to protect and sustain itself; the Selves collectively become the Unconscious-Self. Because of many tribulations and unpleasant experiences, the ego produces hateful, angry and vindictive Selves, to name a few. The Earth is a treacherous planet with a very violent past, and most humans have suffered physical torture, violent death and incarceration—these experiences create very dark Selves. During thousands of embodiments, many Selves get created, making the Unconscious-Self stronger; this only deepens the

Conscious-Self's forgetfulness of its connection to its I-AM-Presence. At some point, the Unconscious-Self takes over entirely; the Conscious-Self gets relegated to the background and becomes a mute spectator. The Unconscious-Self also creates the personality which reflects the ego's chronic fears and insecurities.

The Conscious-Self, now oblivious of its divine heritage, completely identifies itself with the Unconscious-Self which always feels powerless, limited and a victim of circumstances. This feeling of helplessness is the state of humanity and is the reason for all struggle, discord and suffering on Earth. When humans act out of fear, insecurity, helplessness and limitations, their thoughts and actions are discordant and violent. In the course of many embodiments, the four lower bodies accumulate a lot of impurities through inharmonious thoughts and actions. These impurities lead to tribulations, such as illnesses, diseases and accidents. When the four lower bodies become contaminated, the light from the I-AM-Presence gets obstructed and cannot flow through the human self to fully manifest perfection in one's life.

Every person should purify their four lower bodies to bring a real and lasting transformation in life. Purification, however, is not a simple task; it is a gradual process that requires effort and patience but is very rewarding. When the four lower bodies are free of the cobwebs of impurities, the Conscious-Self realises its vastness and its connection with something much greater—its I-AM-Presence. Your I-AM-Presence is your true identity that your Conscious-Self, currently dominated by your Unconscious-Self, must reclaim.

If a critical mass of humankind purifies their four lower bodies, a lot of positive changes will happen on Earth.

It is important not to overanalyse the difference between the ego and the Unconscious-Self. For all practical purposes, it is best to regard them as one.

Manifestation and Purification

Manifestation takes place first in the mental body in the form of thoughts, ideas and visualisations; the thoughts charged with emotions from the emotional body, manifest as results on the physical plane. You might wonder if this process is so simple, why is there so much poverty in the world and why do millions go hungry every day. Can't a poor man think and manifest prosperity? The answer is 'No'—it is not that easy. The etheric body gives identity to the individual and colours his or her mental body (thoughts and ideas), emotional body (emotions and feelings) and physical body (actions) in sequence. The poor man's etheric body is a stockpile of memories of past poverty, failures and other tribulations. Unless they purify their etheric body, they will continue to identify themselves as a destitute and stick to this identity. Consequently, their thoughts and emotions will align with the 'poor person' identity. Therefore, even if that person manifests some prosperity, unless they change their identity, their wealth will not last long. Many poor people who won lotteries, lost their money and became more impoverished than they were before winning the lottery. Purification of the etheric body gives more power and better direction to the mental, emotional and physical bodies.

There is another way to explain manifestation. The quality of your consciousness is inversely proportional to the impurities in your four lower bodies. If you tailor a shirt from a dirty cloth piece, the shirt will be dirty too. The same happens when you manifest anything from an impure consciousness. Your impure manifestation does not satisfy and make you happy; it does not fundamentally improve your life. The law of attraction does not guarantee happiness. Often, people manifest worldly success, material possessions and relationships that do not bring them happiness. It is important to purify your consciousness by cleaning your four lower bodies. Consequently, you will gain greater clarity and manifest only that what serves your life's true purpose.

The Threefold Unfed Flame

The unfed flame is the anchor of the I-AM-Presence inside the human body and has three plumes: blue (left), gold (centre), pink (right). This flame is located inside the heart and is the spark that animates the body. The unfed flame is the seat of a person's identity; a person refers to their self by placing their hand on the heart as this is where their flame resides. In the earlier ages (before the Fall of Man), it used to be more prominent and sometimes visible as a mark on the chest. However, as humankind slipped into darkness, this flame reduced in size and is now just about 1/16th of an inch. It is called the unfed flame because it is eternally self-sustaining, so it does not need any fuel at all. This flame is what gives you a human identity.

The blue plume signifies strength and will power, gold and pink stand for wisdom and love respectively. Any task a person undertakes should ideally be done with energy qualified with all the three qualities (strength and willpower, wisdom and love). If even one quality is lacking, the result is a failure or minimal success. A dictator like Hitler had high will power and strength, but no wisdom and love and so created havoc in the world. Many people have high intelligence and understanding, but lack adequate will power to achieve anything significant. Some people have very loving hearts but have little wisdom, so they also achieve minimal success. It is only when all the three qualities impact an undertaking that real success manifests. In most people, the three flames are unbalanced.

It is your sacred duty to fan and expand the unfed flame in your heart by imagination—it yields incredible results. Imagine not just visually, but also feel strongly that the blue, gold and pink flames in your heart are stretching and becoming larger and larger. Feel the holy flame pulsating within your heart. When you expand this celestial flame, it increases the vibratory rate of the electrons of your four lower bodies. Consequently, the impurities accumulated on the electrons of the four lower bodies get dislodged and you radiate more light. People from all faiths keep their place of worship spotless and tidy, but forget that their bodies are temples of the unfed flame. They wilfully defile their bodies with drugs, alcohol and tobacco, thereby diminishing the glow of this most sacred flame. When you expand the unfed flame, you invite your Christ-Self to sit in the throne of your heart—this is true worship. Be aware that this flame has tremendous power and energy, so do not expand it when emotionally disturbed, or else your negative emotions will amplify, and you will create more karma. When you are emotionally disturbed, first use purification techniques (*discussed later*) and then work on expanding the unfed flame.

Your Seven Bodies

I AM Presence (top), Christ-Self (middle), Human-Self (bottom)

The Threefold Unfed flame

CHAPTER 6
Energy Centres

We know from the previous chapter that the I-AM-Presence animates the physical body through a stream of electrons known as the 'Silver Cord'. This light ray comprises the seven rays (each ray has a distinct colour) that make up the material universe. Seven energy centres known as chakras, distribute the energy from the I-AM-Presence throughout the body. The chakras are in the etheric body of every human being and line along the spinal column. Clean and open chakras are vital for good health and well-being. A chakra clogged with impure energies becomes unbalanced and results in diseases and misfortunes.

Each chakra acts as a distribution centre for a particular ray. There is another chakra (very few people know about it) known as the 'secret heart chakra' into which the light from the I-AM-Presence first enters. From this chakra, the light flows to the heart chakra and from there it gets distributed all over the body through other chakras. Impure feelings in the heart chakra mean that at the very entrance the energy sent by the I-AM-Presence gets polluted and poisons the body. This contaminated energy gets distributed all over the body resulting in diseases, illnesses and misfortunes. The heart chakra is the central chakra, and it is vital to feel love and harmony in the heart.

I briefly describe the chakras below in order of the rays. Every ray is more active on a certain day of the week which is also mentioned.

Throat Chakra

Ray: First ray (Electric Blue)
Day: Tuesday

This chakra is located in the throat and is the seat of will power, energy, drive, communication and sense of timing.

Signs of balance: activeness, results-oriented attitude, being a person of action, ability to rule and manage, good listening abilities, etc.

Signs of imbalance: lying, misusing power, engaging in power plays and politics, lacking hope, fear of trying out unfamiliar things, suppressing creativity and fear of speaking.

Crown Chakra

Ray: Second ray (Golden Yellow)

Day: Sunday

This chakra is located at the top of the head (crown region) and symbolises wisdom, knowledge, illumination, higher consciousness, limitlessness and connectedness with the universe.

Signs of balance: deep seated feeling that everything in Creation is interconnected, ability to derive spiritual wisdom out of any experience, guidance from higher powers, etc.

Signs of imbalance: closed-mindedness, the surety that one is right and the other person is wrong, cynicism or even an obsession with spiritual matters, clinical approach to everything (intellectualism), fanatical attitude, and disconnectedness from the body.

Heart Chakra

Ray: Third ray (Pink)

Day: Monday

This chakra is located in the heart region and is the seat of love, compassion, mercy, selflessness and other virtues.

Signs of balance: unconditional love for others and also oneself, feeling connected to other people and all life, appreciation of beauty, and more.

Signs of imbalance: lacking love, vindictiveness, very conditional love that can also be possessive, feelings of 'end justifies the means', feeling withdrawn and closed from other people, etc.

Base Chakra
Ray: Fourth ray (Brilliant White)
Day: Friday

This chakra is located at the base of the spine. The base chakra is the seat of purity, hope, grounding, self-discipline, security, safety, physical identity and grounding. Most people have an imbalance in this chakra and thus are insecure.

Signs of balance: feeling secure and grounded, knowing that the purpose of life is not to trapped in material desires and bodily needs but to grow in consciousness.

Signs of imbalance: insecurity, greed, living on survival mode only, negativity and lust.

Third-Eye Chakra
Ray: Fifth ray (Emerald Green)
Day: Wednesday

This chakra is located in the centre of the forehead between the eyebrows. The third-eye chakra is associated with intuition, wisdom, truth, psychic abilities and creativity.

Signs of balance: clear-mindedness, a balanced approach to life, inner guidance, synchrony between both sides of the brain, seeing beyond dualities, and the ability to understand the true reasons behind all events and situations.

Signs of imbalance: losing touch with reality, fantasising, critical of other people's point of views, getting stuck with temporary appearances, rejecting spirituality and higher realities, not being able to discern truth and lacking clarity.

Solar Plexus Chakra
Ray: Sixth ray (Purple and Gold)
Day: Thursday

This chakra is located in the stomach area of the body; it is the seat of confidence, personal power, self-esteem, will power and self-discipline.

Signs of balance: warm personality that attracts others, good arbiters and can persuade others to arrive at a consensus, assertiveness and so on.

Signs of imbalance: micromanaging people and situations, lacking ambition and drive, being manipulative, anger and aggression, acting out of rage, not taking a stand, etc.

Soul Chakra

Ray: Seventh ray (Violet)

Day: Saturday

This chakra is located just below the navel and is associated with feeling, emotion, sexuality, creativity and so forth.

Signs of balance: positive attitude towards life, living in the present, carefree and playful attitude, not given to worrying, and more.

Signs of imbalance: sexual obsession, seeing life as a struggle, emotionalism, insensitivity to life, addictions, etc.

Technique for Cleaning Chakras

If you want to clean your throat chakra, then preferably on Tuesday, sit in a quiet place where you are undisturbed. Imagine and strongly feel a tube of electric blue light passing through your throat region and blowing away all impurities from that chakra. You can even imagine a ball of blue light in your throat region, removing all impurities.

You can do the same for all the chakras by imagining the colour of the ray associated with that chakra. It is preferable to clean a chakra on the day associated with the colour of the ray, however it is not necessary. E.g. it is advisable to clean your heart chakra with pink light on a Monday but you can do it on any other day also.

There is another spiritual technique *(explained later in the book)* which is also very effective in cleaning the chakras. The process of cleaning, opening and balancing the chakras takes some time, so do not expect immediate results. Please do not ever force your chakras to open; never use aggression and haste in any spiritual technique.

---

1) Some systems describe chakras in different colours than the one mentioned above, and that is also correct. However, in this book, the chakras are denoted according to the colours of the seven rays.
2) The seven chakras described above are the major chakras, but there are many more.

CHAPTER 7
Duality Consciousness

Duality consciousness is a concept that should be understood by all who seek to expand their consciousness. It is also known as the anti-Christ Consciousness and is the root cause of all evil on our planet. Humankind fell into duality consciousness because it lost touch with its divine origins—this is the 'Fall of Man' as referred in the book of Genesis. In an earlier chapter, I have explained how the Conscious-Self creates the ego that, in turn, creates Selves that collectively form the Unconscious-Self. The ego, Unconscious-Self and personality are always fearful and insecure.

The ego gets a fragmented view of life because it sees everything through the perception filters of personality, religion, culture and beliefs. It perceives others as enemies or rivals who are out to destroy or rob it; it even sees Mother Nature as its enemy that should be fought against and conquered. The ego often creates imaginary enemies—it feels there is always an enemy out there. Being full of fear and insecurity, the ego is always reactive and seeks to control others; it will do anything to defend itself. For the ego, nothing is ever enough and it always thinks there is a scarcity of resources, wealth and abundance, so it must snatch all these from others even through violent means. The consciousness of most people is ego-dominated and fragmented by their perception filters. Therefore, they get a distorted and incomplete picture of reality, and this state of consciousness is called duality consciousness.

Every human being and every single aspect of life on Earth is afflicted with duality consciousness. 'Duality', as the term itself suggests, creates opposites such as good and evil, right and wrong, justified and unjustified—this is how the majority of human beings view life. Duality consciousness actuates humans to instigate divisions and conflicts on the basis of religious or racial prejudices; use force and violence to control and acquire power over others; gain wealth by exploitation of humans and natural resources; be judgmental of other people; etc. A person deep in duality consciousness is likely to have a divisive, perhaps also a destructive, mindset and be very prejudiced. Such a person prefers to see only a partial view of a situation.

Some manifestations of duality consciousness are as follows:

- **Polarity of right and wrong** - We see this everywhere—how every individual, organisation, religion, political party and sect has its own self-centred and selfish views on right and wrong. This right-wrong consciousness has led to all wars (border, civil, religious and so forth), religious fanaticism, exploitation of the poor by the wealthy, environmental destruction and other evils that plague humankind.

- **Polarity of extremes** - Humans, both as individuals and groups, have a proclivity to go to extremes. In politics we have left-wing and the right-wing, communists and capitalists, radicals and conservatives, and more. We see that these groups with opposing ideologies are continuously clashing and fighting each other—there is never an end to their bickering. Even in an individual's life, when something does not work out, they often go to the extreme opposite. E.g. if a false spiritual teacher exploits a sincere spiritual student, the latter often assumes that all teachers are charlatans, and spirituality is a sheer waste of time. They often rush into a sensation-seeking life and become depraved.

- **Polarity of strong and weak** - One of the worst manifestations of duality consciousness is the idea of strong and weak. Those in positions of wealth and power consider it their birthright to rule over the poor and the weak. Instead of trying to uplift the latter, they try to dominate them and tragically succeed most of the time. How else does one explain that a significant portion of the world's wealth is in the hands of few people while millions go to sleep on an empty stomach? Why do powerful countries attack the weaker ones and loot their resources, and even then their gargantuan appetites are never full? Even in human relationships, many, especially marriages, break down because the 'stronger' person dominates the 'weaker'.

Apart from the ones mentioned above, there are other polarities such as atheism vs theism, theism vs rationalism, scientific materialism vs religion, pro-blacks vs anti-blacks and liberals vs conservatives. Such polarities have created conflicts that have caused an immeasurable loss of lives in wars and riots, environmental destruction and so on. Only superficially it looks that these conflicts have made humankind progress, but it is not so. The destruction caused by these polarities far outweighs the benefits. Wars happen due to polarity of thought between warring nations, and humankind could have made progress even without the killing of millions of people in wars.

Duality consciousness fragments one's view of a situation by creating polarities. No problem is seen in its totality because every individual sees what they want to see through their perception filters and gets an incomplete picture. Consequently, lasting solutions are never found, so conflicts and violence continue. The only way to prevent this is to expand one's consciousness and not resolve any situation through violence and/or a polarised mind. As your consciousness expands, you will start feeling the unity and interconnectedness of all life. You will see all life on Earth and all Creation as extensions of yourself. You will wonder why, unlike the various parts of your body, the different parts of life, such as countries, governments and religions, do not cooperate with each other. The lesser non-dual state of mind you act from, the more facets of a situation you will see. Take note that, acting from a non-dual state of mind does not mean not taking a stand. It means taking a stand from a higher perspective after having gained a more expansive and unbiased view of the situation—this results in a more holistic and optimal solution. If a critical mass of people transcends their current level of consciousness, many problems in our world will disappear. There is immense untapped potential for life to improve in every aspect on our planet.

Lastly, you may have a question—are not duality consciousness and non-duality consciousness opposites? The answer is 'No' because duality consciousness is the absence of non-duality consciousness, just as darkness is simply the absence of light and not the opposite of light. It is not always that when a person acts from duality consciousness they do something evil; had this been the case, life on Earth would have ended by now. They just act from a limited consciousness, even though their action might be appropriate for them, from a broader perspective, it may not be the best action. Action taken from a non-duality consciousness is from a higher perspective and is in tune with the greater good.

CHAPTER 8
Fallen Beings

Chengiz Khan killed 40 million people, Joseph Stalin killed 20 million people, Hitler killed 6 million Jews and Pol Pot killed 2 million Cambodians. History has many more examples of such tyrant rulers and dictators.

Do you seriously think an average person is capable of such utter ruthlessness and disregard for life? I am sure your answer is a big 'No'. Only a fallen being is capable of such atrocities.

Fallen beings are those humans responsible for most of the evil, mayhem, war and destruction on our planet. They deserve a separate mention because they are a distinct group of human beings and have traits that separate them from other people. Fallen beings are not the original inhabitants of Earth; they have descended from spheres preceding the seventh. A fallen being receives no light or very little light from its I-AM-

Presence. Therefore, it steals energy from other people through manipulation, violence and domination.

I have already described in an earlier chapter how the Creator created the seven spheres.

Every sphere had spiritual teachers, just as we have in our world, who trained and guided the beings in their sphere to ascend to the spiritual realms. Till the third sphere, things were going right; from the fourth sphere, some beings rebelled against their spiritual teachers and became anti-God. These beings fell into anti-Christ or duality consciousness—they became the fallen beings of the later spheres. The fallen ones were convinced that they were superior to the Creator, and that, both the Creator and his laws were flawed. They fell into evil ways and became ineligible to make their ascension. Consequently, they entered the fifth sphere—this was to give them further chances to correct their mistakes, grow spiritually and make their ascension. Nevertheless, this did not happen, and they continued their evil ways, which resulted in their continued descent into the lower spheres. Many fallen beings from the fourth to the sixth sphere descended into the seventh sphere and continue to embody on Earth. Some fallen ones have pulled their minions not as evil as their masters to embody on Earth. The fallen beings should ideally have ascended from their spheres and not embodied on our planet; they are unwanted guests in our world.

The fallen ones, in millions of years spent on the earlier spheres and Earth, have built up a powerful momentum of evil. They have caused immense harm to our planet and continue to do so. These beings are directly or indirectly responsible for the collapse of many earlier civilisations. You may be surprised to learn that many fallen beings have gained prominent positions of power in various fields: organised religions, business, politics, science, media, entertainment, education and crime. Many of them have become presidents, prime ministers, kings & queens, noblemen, religious heads, business tycoons, dictators and so on. There is a power elite in the world that comprises wealthy and powerful fallen beings who want to play God and control the world. All conspiracy theories are not false, though sometimes the fallen beings plant them in the media to frighten the masses and program their minds. Some members of the power elite are well-meaning individuals who think they are doing good to the world.

Some traits of fallen beings:

- They believe that the end justifies the means, so they are ruthless and show no compassion for fellow human beings. Killing millions of people is very easy for them, as long as it serves their diabolical ambitions.

- They seek power over others and have an endless urge to control people and situations. To acquire control, they manipulate to the maximum extent–they are masters of manipulation. Many religious leaders, cult leaders, priests and clergymen throughout history were fallen beings who corrupted the actual teachings of masters, such as Buddha and Jesus. Organised religions imbibed the debased teachings to manipulate people by injecting fear and guilt in them through rituals, superstitions and beliefs. These fallen beings are the real cause of wars, religious hatred, fanaticism and terrorism. Both the world wars were caused by the same global elite who supported and financed both sides and gained an advantage. The fallen ones who control economies orchestrate recessions by manipulating financial institutions, stock markets and currency, to name a few. It is the global elite that creates problems to frighten people and then offer solutions that slowly but steadily limit the freedom of the people. The people voluntarily give up their freedom under the illusion of 'being offered protection' created by the elite. The fallen beings have manipulated people in more ways than you can imagine.

- The fallen ones are at a very low level of consciousness and have a very narrow view of everything. To them only their own point of view matters, and often they impose it on others by very aggressive means. They believe only what they want to believe. They are also adept at creating compartments within the human mind. One part of the mind believes the opposite of what another part believes, but both parts function well individually. An example–many senior Nazi officers killed people (including children) in the most brutal way possible. Still, when they went back home, they were loving husbands and fathers. You will see that in organised religions, people are devout towards the God of their religion, but are scornful towards the God of other faiths. This is also compartmentalisation because most people from all faiths inwardly accept that there is only one God. Therefore, the question of 'my God' and 'your God' should not even arise. However, in reality, this is not so because the fallen ones have brainwashed people into seeking divisions where none exist.

- They are anti-God, and many think they are superior to God. They have a powerful desire to convince humankind that God's design of the universe and His laws are both imperfect. They think they can manage the Earth better than God; thus, they seek to become God themselves. Their obsession with playing God is the reason the global elite is obsessed with population control and are always conniving to reduce the population of the Earth by various means. Many fallen beings are behind the climate change movement; their intent is to prove that people are responsible for pollution. By blaming people, they want to evade responsibility for polluting the planet in every way possible due to their insatiable greed. These beings use every sector of the economy to further their agenda of playing God and have spread their tentacles into every area of life.

- The fallen beings have a terrible fear of humankind growing in awareness; awakened people will never submit themselves to manipulation and control. Therefore, the fallen ones created religions and corrupted the actual teachings of the prophets. They hid the real Creator God and created a false God for people to worship and remain in spiritual darkness.

- Rapacious ambition, extreme selfishness and ruthless opportunism are three of the most prominent traits of fallen beings. These people believe that everything in this world exists only to serve them, and it is their divine birthright to lord over other people. Fallen beings want majority of the world's population to remain poor. Some leading tycoons in the world were fallen beings who ruthlessly exploited natural resources to enrich themselves. The rape of natural resources is the reason why Nature is in an unbalanced state today. Such is their ambition that fallen beings seek to profit even from the misery of other people; nothing is sacred to them.

- They have a divisive and destructive mindset and are always seeking to break up a country;

create conflicts between religions, races, science and religion, men and women; etc. Many fallen beings work actively against their own country.

- The fallen beings are masters at creating false standards and then forcing humanity to follow them as if these standards were divine. Some standards set by them are pursuing a worldly life and chasing money is more important than seeking spiritual growth; time is money; the wealthy and the powerful should own most of the wealth and resources; one can attain God only by following the outer path of organised religion and blindly obeying the priests; it is honourable to kill people in the name of patriotism, religion, honour or some other so-called epic cause.

- Inducing fear in the masses is one of the primary goals of the fallen beings. They pursue this goal with utter ruthlessness through the media. Many powerful ones own media houses or have high stakes in them. Consequently, most news all over the world that the media churns out is very negative. Humans have become addicted to negativity. In 2014, when the Russian newspaper, 'The

City Reporter' published only good news for just one day, it lost two-thirds of its readers! Many journalists have become merchants of negativity. If the masses live in fear, they can be easily controlled and made to depend on their 'saviours', the fallen beings. The fallen ones use media-induced fear to manipulate religions, countries and ethnic groups into fighting each other. Consequently, as warring parties remain distracted, in the background the fallen ones continue giving shape to their nefarious plans.

The above traits are much more prominent in a fallen being as compared to an average individual. However, every person who possesses some or all of them is not necessarily a fallen being. Everyone in the world is affected by the fallen consciousness; therefore, it is not wise to make a hasty judgment and label someone a fallen being. Not every person who acquires wealth, power and prestige falls in this unholy category; many are sincere, talented and hard-working individuals. Fortunately, barely about 2% of the world's population comprises fallen beings. Still, this minority wants to rule the world forever; they have successfully forced, manipulated and bribed many people (original inhabitants of Earth) into serving them. These dark beings have minions everywhere.

It may surprise you, but many fallen beings had attained high spiritual growth in their original spheres; they subsequently lost their wisdom. Their spiritual attainment resulted in them having charismatic personalities in their earthly embodiments. Their charisma enabled them to sway millions of people towards their way of thinking. Adolf Hitler is a textbook example of such a fallen being. Also, a fallen being can be from any walk of life; an ordinary person, not holding wealth and power, can also be a fallen being. Generally, the higher their position in life is, the more the above-mentioned traits they possess. Nevertheless, they generally camouflage their true nature to create a façade of being good people—brazen individuals such as Idi Amin are exceptions, however.

It is very, very difficult to change the fallen beings; rarely does a fallen being moves towards God. Humankind can defeat them only by raising its consciousness. As humans start vibrating at a higher frequency, these beings will begin to disappear permanently from our planet. In the past, many fallen ones have been removed from our planet and no longer embody on Earth.

The Fall of Man

Before the advent of the fallen beings, the Earth was an extraordinarily beautiful planet with glowing translucent matter and perfect climatic conditions. There were no diseases, vermin and natural disasters on the planet. Perfection reigned on Earth, and human bodies were beautiful, graceful and robust. The threefold flame in the heart was much bigger than it is now. Legends of such times appear in some ancient texts and inscriptions—the book of Genesis describes that period as the 'Garden of Eden'. The first three root races of humans inhabited the Earth in succession. Since our planet was in pristine condition, each root race made its ascension within the 14,000 years allotted to it. The period during the time of the first three root races was known as the 'Golden Ages'.

However, the days of perfection did not last beyond the third root race because along with the fourth root race, the fallen beings started to embody on Earth and brought evil with them. These dark beings polluted the consciousness of humankind on Earth ('Fall of Man' as described in the book of Genesis), and the planet's energies became dense. Purity and innocence were now memories only; humans forgot the Creator. Human nature started manifesting cunningness, dishonesty, gossiping and other discordant traits. Imperfections in the form of diseases, blight, pestilence and natural disasters started to appear on Earth. Because of the fallen consciousness, the evolution of the current root race of humans has been considerably delayed.

The fallen consciousness brought by the fallen beings caused incalculable damage to the Earth—our beloved planet continues to suffer to this day.

The Fall of Man also resulted in the higher realms becoming invisible to humans. Till the end of the third Golden Age, the third eye was very active in most humans because of their pure natures and bodies. As a result, most humans possessed highly developed psychic abilities: clairvoyance, clairaudience, clairsentience and more. They could see other realms, communicate with higher beings and had a very expanded view of reality. Even the five senses of sight, touch, hearing, taste and smell were far more refined than they are now. As humans became impure both in nature and body, their highly developed powers of mind and five senses started to dim. This is the reason that human senses today are less developed than those of most animals! Our limited senses allow us to see only a small fraction of the surrounding reality. Consequently, most of humankind thinks that there is nothing beyond the material universe. The truth is that the entire material universe is tiny compared to the spiritual realms! There are realities so vast that humanity can scarcely comprehend.

Every human being has a third eye, the seat of which is the pineal gland. The third eye connects humans to higher realms and dimensions. Individuals with awakened third eyes can see auras, feel energies, see higher realities and have well developed psychic powers. After the Fall of Man, the pineal gland became covered with impure substances; thus, humankind lost one of the most precious gifts of the Creator. A shell of impurity covers the pineal gland in most people today, and this is because of many reasons: chemicals in water and packaged food products; pesticides, herbicides, excessive calcium or mercury in various products; alcohol and tobacco; etc. The hard cover on the pineal gland blocks access to the third eye; as a result, humanity cannot see beyond the material world. Humanity is like a frog that is content living inside a well, so does not bother to explore the world outside the well. The fallen beings and their minions do not, under any circumstances, want humankind to reactivate their third eye.

Just as they have used religion, the fallen beings are now using scientific materialism to mislead and confuse people. Scientific materialism aims to make people believe that there is nothing beyond the material universe and that higher realities do not exist. This diabolical distortion of truth suits the fallen beings very well. It furthers their agenda of imposing their standards on humankind to keep it under their control. If people come to know of higher laws of

Creation, they will no longer follow the false standards of the fallen beings. Please do not give credence to misleading theories that we live in a digitally simulated or virtual reality world as shown in the 'Matrix' movies, and that every human being is a computer program. Such theories only intend to trap humanity in matter consciousness. Every lifestream is a spark of the Creator and thus is a son or daughter of God.

CHAPTER 9

The Sinister Force

Before I explain what the sinister force is, I would like you to know that thoughts are things and have colour. An angry thought is red coloured, a love thought is of pink colour and so on. Thoughts are energies so are not visible to the human eye. When a person thinks, a thought-form is created. A weak thought-form dissipates faster than a stronger thought-form. Human beings are constantly creating thought-forms that travel far and wide. Therefore, a person who intensely contemplates suicide releases a thought-form that can influence someone in another country to commit suicide, irrespective of whether the former kills oneself. Likewise, a strong positive thought travels far and influences others. The mental world of all human beings is one; it is like a multi-plug where the connecting individual plugs are humans.

The sinister force is the effluvia of evil and negativity all around us and exists because of both human and non-human reasons. It is a potent living entity that seeks to harm humankind and prevent the spiritual awakening of people. The fallen beings are the reason for the sinister force originating on Earth. The fallen consciousness made the thoughts of human beings impure. Since the Fall of Man, the sinister force has been gathering momentum thanks to the negativity generated by humans. Therefore, we see that God has not created evil, so He is not responsible for it.

The sinister force reaches up to a height of approx. 8000 feet from the Earth's surface. Consequently, while flying at 35000 feet in an aeroplane, one has lesser and weakened impure thoughts. Perhaps now you understand why people living in high-altitude regions are usually not as cunning, sly and manipulative as those living in the lowlands. In ancient times, monasteries were built in mountains so that the monks there could meditate with minimal disturbance from the sinister force.

The sinister force comprises two types of entities: Carnates and Discarnates.

- **Carnates** - These are thought-forms charged with negative emotions of anger, hatred and fear that humans are unceasingly creating and releasing in the psychic atmosphere of the Earth. The carnates float in the atmosphere and affect people, including the person who created it. Some carnates, especially those charged with anger, are so hideous that their human creator would freeze in terror if they could see them. The carnates contribute a tremendous amount of negativity to our planet.

Psychic Mobs

Since many people are on the Internet, I think it necessary to inspect what I call 'Psychic Mobs'. We all know that a mob is a group of violent people who create havoc on the streets. Mobs are not just physical mobs, there are psychic mobs as well. Psychic mobs are groups of people active on the Internet through social media, internet forums and online communities. Every group supports a political party, ideology, religion, country or a cause. Group members who post articles, tweets and responses charged with anger, hatred and vindictiveness, generate negative thought-forms. Millions of people are doing this every day on the Internet and have become addicted to it. Every day they get up and get their daily fix of negativity from the Internet.

- **Discarnates** - Discarnates are the ghosts of people who have died. Many people, because of wrong living, worldly attachments, premature or violent deaths and lack of spiritual growth, cannot move into the spiritual realm after their deaths. Consequently, they remain stuck in the vibratory region of the Earth. A dead person can also linger due to emotional attachment with their buried corpse; cremation is always preferable because the physical body ceases to exist. Discarnates inhabit places with low and dense vibrations: graveyards, bars, brothels, hospitals, and gambling dens, to name a few. They mostly get attracted to humans whose energy fields are weak because of the accumulation of negative emotions. Most people are not aware of how much distress discarnates cause in their lives.

How the Sinister Force Harms Humankind

<u>Harming an Individual</u>

- A carnate released by a person not only harms the human target but always, without fail, boomerangs on the sender; it attacks their emotional body. A person who habitually generates impure thought-forms of fear, anger, jealousy and hatred, inevitably attracts diseases, illnesses and misfortunes. Thoughts of violence and anger cause fatigue. Observe yourself the next time you harbour negative thoughts; you will feel drained of energy. Impure energies in the energy field of a person can weaken the aura and create holes in the auric field. These holes invite discarnate entities to attach themselves to the person.

- A discarnate attaches itself to the aura of its victim and starts to feed upon the person's energy. If not removed, it can disrupt and ruin its victim's life completely. It can even possess a person's body—a term we call 'possession'. Discarnates, almost always, influence the behaviour of the person they get attached to and cause failure in relationships, business losses, diseases, accidents, suicidal or homicidal thoughts, etc. Some signs of a discarnate attachment are tiredness, irritation and rage, sickness, accelerated ageing, loss of blood, weak physique and so forth. Often, these entities cause or exacerbate mental illnesses and make mentally ill people babble to themselves or manifest other abnormalities.

Frequently, discarnates incite even regular people into committing crimes and other wrongful actions. These entities trouble not just individuals but also organisations, including corporates. Many business deals have fallen through or gone wrong because of discarnates.

- There are many 'cursed' spots on Earth that attract mishaps, accidents and other unfortunate events. These spots are often inhabited by several carnates and discarnates. Till the time these entities disappear from that spot, mishaps continue to happen there.

Harming Humanity

The sinister force sustains and energises the Unconscious-Selves of all human beings and vice versa. This self-sustaining cycle is what prevents evil from disappearing from the world. The Unconscious-Selves of humankind have polluted the mass consciousness with selfishness, anger, fear and hatred. The sinister force has permeated every area of life: education, entertainment, religion & spirituality, business, politics and governance. It is not surprising that Earth is such a dark planet. There is not one person on this planet who is not affected by the sinister force; therefore, spiritual protection is a must for everyone.

Besides the above-mentioned facets of life, the sinister force inflicts tremendous suffering on human beings through the fury of Mother Nature *(this is discussed in the next chapter 'Why Nature Rebels?')*

To sum it up, entities are all around us, but just because you do not see them, it does not mean they do not exist. It is a wonder that some 'modern' minded people and so-called rationalists do not believe in entities because they cannot see them. How come they believe in the existence of microwaves that enable their wireless gadgets, gases, bacteria and other invisible phenomena?

I will, however, end this chapter on a positive note. Just as humans generate negative thought-forms, they also generate positive thought-forms of joy, happiness, love and positivity. To that end, festivals and celebrations, loving and authentic relationships, family gatherings, high-quality and wholesome entertainment are necessary. Though many people are awakening spiritually, diabolical forces are still dominant. Therefore, more people should raise their consciousness to defeat evil.

The sudden cataclysms that occur in nature, creating havoc and mass injury, are not "acts of God".
Such disasters result from thoughts and actions of man.
Whenever the world's balance of good and evil is disturbed by an accumulation of harmful vibrations, the results of man's wrong thinking and wrong doing, you will see devastation.
— Paramhansa Yogananda

CHAPTER 10
Why Nature Rebels?

Humans do not realise how closely human life is connected with Mother Nature, how the universe acts as a mirror that reflects what we humans project upon it. Therefore, few people fully comprehend how the sinister force affects Nature and the magnetic field of the Earth.

It is common knowledge by now that the human body comprises four elements: earth, air, water and fire. The four elements are conscious beings and revolt in the form of diseases and illnesses when relentlessly assaulted with discordant thoughts of anger, fear, violence and hatred. Now extend this logic a little. If the four elements of the human body can revolt through diseases, why can't these elements that are present also in Nature, revolt? Humans are unceasingly polluting the psychic atmosphere of the Earth with inharmonious thoughts that adversely affect the four elements in Nature. When toxicity released by humans crosses a limit, Nature rebels in the form of natural disasters such as floods, tsunamis, and earthquakes. Deserts exist because of the dryness in emotions and lack of love in human beings. Mother Nature, just as a human mother, is loving and nurturing, but she cannot tolerate humankind's misbehaviour indefinitely. Unless humans expand their consciousness and generate harmonious thoughts of love, cooperation and mutual understanding, natural disasters will continue.

The scientific community is unlikely to accept the above-stated truth as it is trapped in scientific materialism and is too arrogant even to want to look beyond it. Even the most sophisticated instruments cannot tap into the higher laws that govern the universe. Instruments can detect changes in the Earth's vibration and warn of earthquakes; however, they can never detect the deeper causes behind earthquakes. One might argue that shifts in the tectonic plates cause earthquakes. Sure, but what is the energy that causes the movement of the plates? It is the collective negative energy of humans on Earth! Only by raising one's consciousness can one gain insights into the higher laws of the universe. Thousands of years ago, sages in

India discovered truths and universal laws that would baffle many people today, including those from the scientific community.

The polluted energies of the Earth are also responsible for the existence of vicious and harmful forms of life, such as vermin and venomous animals. The wicked thoughts that humans release reflect back as vicious life-forms on Earth. This is the reason why cockroaches, rats, locusts, mosquitoes, scorpions, etc., exist on our planet.

Though humans are more evolved than animals, in many ways, animals have a far greater understanding of Nature than humans. In the Tsunami that occurred in 2004, millions of people died while almost no animal or perhaps very few died. Animals sensed the disaster far ahead of humans and their sophisticated instruments, and ran away from or avoided the disaster zones. Since, unlike humans, animals do not harm Nature, they are gifted with higher extrasensory perception to protect themselves from her fury. This does not mean that animals never die in natural disasters; they do perish when they are trapped and cannot escape. However, it is a truth that they can sense natural disasters far better than humans.

The Elementals

Creation is infinitely vast, complex and mysterious. Humankind still knows very little about the Earth, let alone the higher aspects of Creation. Most people are entirely unaware of the many forces that are working to sustain life on Earth.

Most people do not care to look beyond the world of matter and ignore all higher realities. If you are one such person, ask yourself, what created you? You are here because of your parents, and they existed because of your grandparents. Think over this—why does your wooden computer table exist? It exists because of the tree that provided the wood and the carpenter who constructed it. The table cannot be higher than the carpenter.

Likewise, you must have created many things in your life, such as a business, painting or an invention, but none of your creations is greater than you. You are higher than all that you have created or will create in the future. In conclusion, anything that exists as a form is created by something higher than it—our planet Earth is no exception. Indeed, it is a creation of seven beings known as the Elohim. This book will not discuss in detail about the Elohim. Suffice for you to know that they are higher than the ascended masters and have powers to create planets. Perhaps in organised religions, they are known by different names.

The Elohim created the material universe and the four realms: etheric, mental, emotional and physical. Just as factories need workers, the four realms also require workers to build and sustain the structures in those realms. Therefore, the Elohim created the elemental beings out of their light; each realm has its elemental beings. The Earth, being a part of the physical realm of the material universe, has elemental beings for each of the four elements: fire elementals, air elementals, water elementals and earth elementals. The elementals are conscious beings but lack self-awareness; they mimic and mirror back whatever they see. Paracelsus, a great Swiss physician, alchemist, philosopher and lay theologian, was one of the first persons to talk about elemental beings.

Earlier in this chapter, we learnt humankind's impure thoughts harm Nature and how the four elements on Earth rebel. Going deeper into this phenomenon, we learn that it is the elemental beings in those elements that cry out in pain. Humankind can scarcely imagine how much pain it inflicts on these tiny beings when it poisons the Earth through filth, pollution and impure thoughts. Burial of dead bodies is one of the worst things that humans do to the elementals. Can you imagine how much the elementals on our planet suffer when putrid corpses and carcasses rot and stink in their midst? The earth elementals have no choice but to decompose the bodies. Cremation is advisable because fire is a great purifier that consumes everything without causing agony to the earth elementals.

All life-forms desire to evolve and elementals are no exception. Elementals often choose animal bodies for their evolution. Unlike humans, animals living in their natural habitat have group souls, so if a wild deer dies, its soul gets merged into the group soul of all Deer. Consequently, the same exact soul cannot re-embody just as it not possible to get the same molecules after having poured water from a spoon back into the glass. The situation with animals that live in proximity with humans is different. The elementals know that living with humans hastens their evolution; this is why they often inhabit the bodies of pets; this is the reason pets develop an individuality or a personality. Since elementals mimic and reflect what they see, often pet dogs resemble their masters. Many pets often behave like humans—thousands of videos on the Internet prove this. The elemental inside your pet's body has entered your life to evolve into something higher, so do not treat your pet as an accessory. If your pet exhibits timidity or any other behavioural flaw, it becomes your spiritual duty to help it overcome that imperfection. Often, when a pet dies, the elemental of that pet, drawn by love, returns to the owner through another pet. If the new pet displays traits of the earlier pet, the owner thinks the earlier pet has re-embodied.

Elementals can evolve beyond animals; many people closely attuned to Nature are reincarnations of elementals. Some environmentalists and Nature lovers are incarnated elementals. However, unless an elemental obtains the threefold unfed flame, it cannot embody as a human.

The Body Elemental

Every human being, right before its first embodiment, is provided with an elemental being—the body elemental. This elemental friend accompanies the human in every embodiment until the human's ascension. The body elemental, under the supervision of the I-AM-Presence, creates the four lower bodies (etheric, emotional, mental and physical) of the human in every embodiment. These bodies are the vehicles for the incoming soul for its sojourn on Earth. The process of creation of a human body is very complex, so the body elemental has to have a developed consciousness. The body elemental lives in the etheric realm and is about three feet tall—it is a replica of its human. Besides creating the four bodies, this elemental also performs the natural body functions and keeps control of the human till about the age of twelve (it can be till twenty-one also) when after that the Christ-Self takes over. Since the elementals mimic, often children copy their elders.

During the first three Golden Ages, when the Earth was pure, and humans did not generate discordant feelings, the body elemental used to happily cooperate with the higher powers to create perfect and beautiful human bodies. However, after the fall of humankind, the Earth became a dark planet and humankind's thoughts became impure. The body elemental became bewildered but obediently kept building the human bodies with the raw material of bad karma and impure feelings of the human. Thus, the human bodies created after the third Golden Age are not as beautiful and robust as those from earlier ages. The continued impurity thrust upon it by humans has made the body elemental irritable. Therefore, it no longer sees its human companion as a friend, so no longer cooperates as before. It rarely helps in healing and leaves the human to fend for itself.

The four lower bodies innately contain the blueprint of perfection that manifested fully during the Golden Ages. The blueprint is no longer evident on our bodies because it lies buried and forgotten under the impurities and discord of the post-Golden Ages period. To make the four lower bodies pure, one must use spiritual techniques *(discussed later in the book)*. Once the four bodies become pure, the body elemental will again cooperate in making the human body beautiful and disease-free.

CHAPTER 11
Why Religions Decay?

What makes an organised religion decay is something humankind needs to understand because more people die in the name of God than anything else. The actual purpose of religion is to purify humankind's consciousness. Nevertheless, with time, religions become corrupt and instead of liberating people, enslave them and stymie their spiritual growth. Ideally, religion should be a ship that transports an individual from their human self to their divine self; however, the ship always becomes shipwrecked and decays.

How Organised Religions are Formed?

Spiritual masters such as Krishna, Jesus and Buddha come into the world to show humanity a new alternative, a new reference point and a higher way to live. No true master ever forces his teachings upon people, and never condemns anyone who refuses to become a follower. A spiritual master is a sun that shines its light upon people, a light that some accept and some refuse. Every master encourages people to attain the same state of consciousness that the former has attained. No prophet ever desired to create religions or be worshipped by people despite what the scriptures say.

The prophet's passing away becomes a perfect opportunity for various people to create a religion around the former's teachings. This group of people often includes the master's direct disciples or those in the line of succession; fallen beings that may comprise kings, noblemen and politicians; and other ambitious people. They create religions and religious institutions for two reasons: livelihood and power over people. The religion's propounders have no interest in the spiritual growth of the followers because an expanded consciousness would make people intelligent and resistant to control. As a result, the 'holy' custodians distort the actual teachings of the prophet to impede the spiritual growth of the followers. Often, powerful people propagate the religion for political reasons— Roman emperor Constantine's support for Christianity was more because of political convenience than faith. Even if a religion is founded by well-meaning individuals, it eventually gets defiled.

Some Reasons Why Organised Religions Decay

- Once the founder prophet passes on, a power struggle starts amongst the disciples, and more than one disciple wants to become the successor. Politics becomes an integral part of that religion—almost every religious organisation is an epicentre of politics, power struggle, jealousy and ambition. When after the master's passing, politics takes the frontbench, then the religion can only evolve in one way—the political way. The religion, instead of seeking to uplift the people, degenerates into a numbers game; therefore, some religions are aggressive in converting people to their faith through bribes, manipulation and force. In religious organisations, often, the top positions of power are usurped by power-hungry and corrupt individuals who have little interest in the spiritual growth of the members and followers.

- Most of the disciples of the founder prophet are not as spiritually developed as their master and do not fully comprehend the master's teachings. Among Jesus's disciples, John 'the beloved' was the only one almost fully attuned to his master. When the disciples teach the masses, they seldom convey the true essence of the teachings. Many senior disciples who were close to the prophet establish their own sects, and every sect claims to correctly interpret the prophet's teachings. Some sects even claim exclusive rights on the teachings while others distort the teachings to suit their own agenda.

- Translation of the original teachings into other languages is another reason for the teachings getting distorted. The translators often add their own interpretations, perhaps with no ulterior motives; the original teachings partially lose their essence. Because of multiple translations, a stage comes when no one knows what the actual truth is. Some scriptures are written in ancient languages that are now extinct, and often errors and misinterpretations happen when they are decoded and translated.

- After the passing away of the founder prophet, the successors camouflage the teachings through doctrines, dogmas, strict rules and regulations. The codified teachings are almost always used to inject fear and guilt in people, make them superstitious and control them. Therefore, the followers never really become free, but become perpetually dependant on their religion's custodians. Some religions impose such strict rules on their followers that they take away the joy from the life of the followers. These rules could be regarding clothing, entertainment and other aspects of daily life; this is suppression, and the outcome is always anger. The suppressed anger manifests as hardened feelings and fanaticism. If you observe, you will realise that many religious people carry anger within themselves. Often, the religious leaders and priests who impose strict rules on the followers, are hypocrites and do not observe the rules they themselves have established. A true master never teaches people to fear God but to love God and obey the universal laws of life. However, many organised religions are fear based and teach people to fear God. They portray God as a wrathful tyrant who unfailingly punishes even those individuals who unintentionally commit a wrong.

- Often, religions expunge essential teachings for purely political reasons. The effacement of the concept of reincarnation (re-embodiment) from Christianity is one such example. When a religion ignores reincarnation, it leaves many questions unanswered. Research done by pioneers such as Dr Ian Stevenson and Dr Raymond Moody has proven beyond doubt the validity of reincarnation. However, orthodox religions continue to adamantly deny reincarnation and forbid their followers from believing in it—this is another control mechanism. The fact is, reincarnation provides a lifestream opportunities to learn from a variety of experiences and also to work out its karma and settle its karmic debts.

- Powerful people in the religion's hierarchy often have their likes and dislikes, fears, eccentricities, prejudices and political affiliations which they force upon their followers. These impositions have no connection with the prophet's teachings and only gratify the egos of powerful people. Some followers get frustrated with the unnecessary diktats and rules and join cults, thereby sinking deeper into spiritual darkness. Unstable and evil individuals, such as Jim Jones and David Koresh, become leaders of various cults. These cults are predatory, fanatical and only seek to enslave their followers.

- Often, even the scriptures are a cause for distortions in the teachings. The prevailing culture and society determine the richness of a language (vocabulary, grammar, semantics, etc.); therefore, the more evolved a civilisation, the richer the language. The vocabulary of their times constrains spiritual masters, such as Jesus and Buddha, so they use metaphors and allegories in their teachings to explain subtle spiritual concepts. The consciousness of the people who came in contact with Jesus was not very developed. Therefore, despite Jesus's best efforts, many people could not understand the metaphors and parables that he used. Most prophets face the challenge of a restrictive vocabulary and the danger of being misunderstood. The worst part is that even in present times while deciphering ancient scriptures, scholars and researchers often interpret the original metaphors too literally and ignore their real meaning. The misinterpretation of teachings gives the priesthood the excuse to impose the distorted rules and rituals upon the followers. You can understand now why one sacred teaching is interpreted in many ways resulting in confusions, arguments and acrimony. Unless a person has reached a certain level of consciousness, they should refrain from reading scriptures because they are likely to misinterpret the symbolism and the metaphors.

- Most organised religions refuse to evolve and continue to emphasise outdated rituals that were probably relevant in bygone eras. A primitive practice like animal sacrifice* is still prevalent in some religions. When people forget their real significance, rituals become mechanical and meaningless. The younger generation, understandably, questions many of the age-old beliefs and dogmas. Organised religions are stuck in time and have become stagnant and no longer fulfil the expectations of the modern age.

- Mysticism is the life of every religion, and when the priesthood rejects it, the religion becomes dry and atrophies. Bereft of mysticism, religion becomes a set of rules, dogmas, doctrines, rituals and sermons by priests that aim to control and exploit the followers. Mysticism is the inner path and teaches meditation, devotion, practising silence and observing one's thoughts. It is spiritual practices, not outdated rituals and sermons by sanctimonious preachers, that improve the spiritual seeker's psychological health by transforming their consciousness. Another outcome of rejecting mysticism is that it often leads to fanaticism. Terrorism is the ugliest manifestation of fanaticism.

- Often, politicians form alliances with influential religious leaders. The reason being that religious figures have numerous followers who will vote for a political party recommended by them. Politics is a dirty business all over the world, and when politics joins hands with religion, how can the latter remain pure? No wonder many religious heads and leaders become corrupt, power-hungry and selfish. The influence of mainstream politics on orthodox religions is also one of the reasons for corruption in religions.

Organised religions, despite all their drawbacks, have played at least a minor part in evolving humanity. However, humanity still has not evolved in consciousness to the extent it should have. Organised religions have utterly failed to eradicate selfishness from humankind's consciousness. Therefore, our world is plagued with vast inequalities of income, environmental destruction and conflicts (political, religious and economic). It is humankind's dire need to step beyond the boundaries of orthodox religion and seek higher truths that demolish humanity's egocentric approach to life.

No true prophet or enlightened master ever propagates sacrificing or hurting a life (animal, another human or even one's own self) to please God. Such blood rituals are thrust upon by custodians of the religion (mostly fallen beings) upon the followers; this is done to keep the followers trapped in low levels of consciousness.

CHAPTER 12
Idolatry Destroys Religion

Organised religions have used idolatry to a great extent to distort the actual teachings of prophets and spiritual masters. The intent behind promoting idolatry is to keep people in spiritual darkness.

The best strategy to prevent people from understanding the teachings of the master is to project him as divine, God-like and perfect. The supernatural image of the master ensures that he goes beyond the reach of people except *seemingly* the priesthood and custodians of the religion. The followers become too awed of the master to even think of following his example; therefore, as an alternative to personally relating to him, they start worshipping him. The cult of worship defeats the very purpose of the master's mission—to show that every person can attain the same level of consciousness as the master. Instead of taking responsibility for themselves and striving towards inner awakening, people become trapped in idolatry—this is the beginning of organised religion.

The creators of the religion elevate themselves to the position of being the official representatives of the prophet and portray themselves as the only direct link between the people and God. Religion then becomes a centre of power, politics and money. From this point onwards, everything starts falling apart. Organised religions force their followers to worship the prophet, believe in him and adhere to outer rules created by the religion's founders. The followers walk on a false path to heaven not realising that the shortcut of worshipping anything external never works. Spiritual progress necessitates taking total responsibility for oneself by purifying one's consciousness.

The following points illustrate how idolatry corrupts religion:

- **Weaving fiction** - The custodians and founders of the religion create myths and legends that vastly exaggerate facts from the prophet's life—the intent is to awe the masses into worshipping the prophet. Often, over-enthusiastic disciples and students add to the myths to make their master more popular. The stories are brought to life through insertions and editions in the original scriptures and holy texts. Various forms of art such as folk songs, drama, paintings and statues also propagate legends about the prophet. One example is the story that as soon as Buddha was born, he walked and seven lotuses appeared for the seven steps he took. It is hilarious to think that a newly born baby would walk! Another story is about Jesus being born of a virgin. The fact is that neither Jesus nor his mother, Mary, ever made any claims about the latter being a virgin when she conceived Jesus. Jesus was born in the same manner as any other human is born. You will find many such fictitious stories in almost every religion. Many of these narratives portray the masters and prophets as super perfect beings who led perfect lives and could do no wrong. The fact is that on the Earth plane, even the greatest of the spiritual masters cannot be perfect. Many spiritual masters had families, property, and lived like any of us. They too faced the day-to-day problems of life and did not perform supernatural feats to overcome them. Like all people, the masters also experienced anger, irritation and frustration. Mary had other children besides Jesus and indeed just like any other mother, she too would often go crazy in dealing with them.

When fiction continues for thousands of years from generation to generation, it goes so deep into the collective psyche of the people that they do not bother to question it. No wonder only a small percentage of people strive seriously for spiritual growth. Most people are content with religious fiction, so do not bother to awaken. Not just in olden days, but even in present times, most people (both literate and illiterate) continue to believe in such religious fiction. The reality is that, the Creator God has no favourites, so it did not create any lifestream as special. All spiritual masters and prophets achieved spiritual mastery by their own efforts, and this is what they try to teach people. No special favours were bestowed upon them by the Creator. The picture that organised religions convey about their founder prophets and masters being perfect and special creations of God is wrong and misleading. While prophets such as Krishna and Jesus performed many miracles, not all stories and escapades stated in the scriptures are true. Many of them have been exaggerated or stated in the wrong context to make the master appear more superhuman and out-of-reach of ordinary people.

- **Distorting the persona** - Jesus never claimed to be the only son of God—this was planted in Christianity by the fallen beings who are always seeking to overawe, intimidate and control people. Jesus, however, did hint that one needs to attain a certain level of consciousness to realise their kinship with God. The Universal Christ Consciousness is the 'only begotten Son of God' and has existed since Creation began; without it, even the Creator could not have formed Creation. The Universal Christ Consciousness manifests in the Christ-Self of every human being as individualised Christ Consciousness. Therefore, upon attaining oneness with their Christ-Self, one becomes a 'Christ' and can be called a son or daughter of God. Christianity used Jesus's attainment of Christ Consciousness as a perfect excuse to elevate him to the super-special status of being the only son of God. The supernatural elevation of Jesus eclipsed his actual teachings. It also implied that other people were lesser mortals who should only pray to Jesus and not dare to follow his example.

The above are some methods of weaving idolatry into religion. Idolatry destroys true religion and benefits only the priesthood. It is about time humankind understood that prophets and masters incarnate among us to awaken us; they do not want us to worship them. If your religion or preacher says that you cannot reach the spiritual heights of the prophets, it is like telling a fourth-grade student that he/she can never become a graduate. Remember, just as Krishna, Buddha and Jesus, you too have the divine spark of the Creator inside you. You are ignorant of this spark, so you mistakenly think you are inferior to them—this is precisely what orthodox religions want.

CHAPTER 13
The False God of Religions

A false God? Can God be false? Yes, absolutely! It is a false God that organised religions, for thousands of years, have programmed humanity to worship. This false God has served the priesthood very well; it is also a fantastic control mechanism used to inject fear and guilt in people. Why do I use the term 'false God'? Because God, as portrayed by organised religions, is just a notion, nothing more.

Have you ever seriously in your life, thought what God meant to you, how intimately you connect with Him and what role He plays in your day-to-day life? Can you honestly say that you know God? Most likely, your answer is 'No' because God, for you, is just a belief but not experience. Your family (that follows a particular religion) taught you about prayers, mantras, rituals, holy shrines and so forth. Society placed a set of concepts inside your mind, and you have conformed to those concepts without questioning them—someone else's beliefs have now become your beliefs. Perhaps you are also made to believe that your religion is superior to all other religions—this is the leading cause of all religious conflicts.

Have you ever asked yourself and your religious leaders and priests that if their god was so powerful, loving and compassionate then why is the world plagued by so much misery, poverty, hatred, unhappiness and selfishness? Why is that during a worldwide calamity such as the Corona pandemic, places of worship of all religions get closed down, and 'God' disappears? Did 'God' become afraid of the Covid virus?

Have you ever wondered why the priests of your religion prattle about brotherhood and love, yet expect you to be cynical of people of other faiths? Why is there so much distrust and violence between different religions? Why most people are still so violent, though more mentally than physically, towards each other? Why do religious organisations hoard billions of dollars collected as donations yet are stingy in serving the poor (unless of course, they are converting poor people to their religion by bribing them with money)? The founder prophets of various religions were true masters and lived humbly. However, in organised religions, we see elaborate hierarchies, costumes and grand titles— have you ever questioned this? Why most priests have no radiance of God's love on their faces and are of very ordinary consciousness like most people in the world? As in regular people, their thoughts also revolve around power, prestige, money and politics. Religious leaders experience jealousy, anger and negative emotions just as most people do, so why place them on a pedestal and give them slavish obedience?

If you observe impartially, you will realise how organised religions create a dependency on an external false God that enslaves people instead of making them take responsibility for themselves. Take note that poor and uneducated people are usually very religious, but the false God they cling to does nothing to alleviate their suffering. In poor countries, governments, hand in glove with religious leaders, 'feed' religion to poor people as a substitute for a decent life.

As an individual, be brutally honest and ask yourself whether worshipping the God of your religion makes you feel good about yourself for most of the day? I am sure 95% of people will reply 'not even twenty minutes a day'. Ponder over this: Has your 'God' freed you from fear, insecurity, anger and other vile emotions? Has your 'God' really connected you to your fellow human beings and Mother Nature? Has your 'God' made you a loving human being who harbours no hatred even for those whose opinions differ from yours? Also, ask yourself why you perform your religious practices: because it is a family tradition, a habit or just a formality. Most people derive no joy in their religious practices—it is just another chore. Had you been genuinely connected to the real God (your I-AM-Presence), you would feel peaceful most of the time, but most people do not feel peaceful. An undercurrent of anger, insecurity and worry always disturbs them. The blunt truth is that the false God of organised religions does nothing to alleviate your suffering or the sufferings of the world.

You can ask yourself many more questions like the ones I have stated above, and if you are fully honest with yourself, the replies will mostly be negative. You will realise that your religious beliefs have given you fake satisfaction and assurances. Why is this so? This is because you were taught the *beliefs* about God, but never taught that you yourself are God individualised but have forgotten your divine origin. No orthodox religion will seriously teach you techniques for expanding your consciousness because then they will lose control over you. They fear your growth in intelligence and realisation of the sheer futility of religious hatred, conversions and other ills that plague all religions. Once you awaken, you will ask questions that organised religions cannot answer—this is why they discourage questions from their followers and expect unquestionable obedience to the most ridiculous of beliefs and rituals. If you were to ask religions about the solution to the world's problems, the silliest reply the priesthood would give is that if the entire world converted to their religion, all of humanity's problems would disappear.

Organised religions have created a false God who is a hotchpotch of theories, mythology, beliefs, traditions, images, emblems, photos, statues, scriptures and rituals—such a 'God' can only be a concept. This 'God' is not the real Creator, just as the photograph of a waterfall is not the waterfall; the false God serves only those for whom religion is a business or a livelihood. The false God of religion is also angry and vindictive and always looking to punish those who disobey him; the real Creator is nothing like this because it is only light and love. It is high time that most people erase the image of the false God from their minds and start marching towards Christhood. Humankind must forsake the juvenile approach to seeking higher truths through orthodox religions.

CHAPTER 14
Religions are Archways

Religions have failed miserably in transforming humanity's consciousness. Human society remains dominated by selfishness, so we continue to see poverty, income inequalities, religious conflicts and environmental destruction. Religions, however, serve one useful purpose—they provide the first step to people who are beginning their spiritual journey.

If you have absolutely no knowledge of higher truths, then the outer path of religion comprising rituals, festivals, pilgrimages, scriptures and hymns is the first step for you. Religious rituals (some are pretty weird and absurd) may give you a glimpse of higher realities and a higher power that has created the world. Also, certain rituals increase the energy levels in the physical body to some extent and give some benefit; however, stagnation sets in after a certain point.

Organised religions cannot make people mature because they do not change the psychology of a person. Often, a very religious individual remains the same person throughout his or her life. The outer path of religion does not transform your consciousness. You may change your jobs, get a new partner, buy more material possessions but when discord, conflicts and tribulations happen, you will continue battling them through your reactionary Unconscious-Self—the same issues will keep repeating in your life. Consequently, your life will remain the same. Furthermore, most people practice religion only because, it is their family tradition; out of habit, greed and fear; to conform and appear respectable.

Many guilt-ridden people donate lots of money to religious organisations hoping it will wash their sins—this is childish. Many wealthy and accomplished people think they are extra close to God, and God is especially favourable towards them—this is again a silly belief. People gain wealth and success because of their actions and talents. Many people quickly acquire vast wealth because they have built up a strong wealth-acquiring karmic momentum from their previous embodiments. Same goes for other talents such as singing and painting. A person might be wealthy, accomplished and respected but spiritually a baby; on the other hand, a humble janitor may possess tremendous spiritual insight. This fact may hurt the egos of many people, but it is the truth. Material success is not an accurate measure of a person's spiritual stature. Some of the greatest sages in the world have lived humble lives, but inwardly they have experienced the bliss and peace that all the money in the world cannot buy. Such people are the real billionaires!

Humans have two types of intelligences: material and spiritual. Many religious people are very materially accomplished; their material intelligence increases with worldly success; thus, with growth in material wealth they become more wordly-wise, manipulative and cunning. Nevertheless, very rarely such people grow in spiritual intelligence that actuates them to transcend their current level of consciousness and be of greater service to society.

It is possible that, like millions of people, you have made some headway in religion but are now stuck. You need to realise that organised religion is the nursery class in your evolution, so no matter how faithful you are to it, you need to move beyond it to enter higher classes. The higher classes are about purifying your four lower bodies, resolving your psychological issues, removing blockages from your chakras and silently observing your thoughts. All this will serve to purify and expand your consciousness; this is a process and involves spiritual techniques, and there is no shortcut to this.

Religions are beautiful archways, but archways nevertheless. The problem is that millions of people are now crowding the several archways, resulting in continuous religious conflicts. Only a small percentage of the world's population seeks to enter the inner sanctum of spiritual growth. Therefore, only a small percentage of humankind has attained a desirable level of consciousness that can raise the collective consciousness of the planet. If you are a spiritual neophyte, you may find it hard to believe that your spiritual growth affects the collective consciousness of humankind on Earth. When you move up in the ladder of consciousness, you exert an upward pull on the consciousness of all humankind. The more the number of spiritually evolved people on Earth, the faster the planet evolves, and the more harmonious life on Earth becomes. You owe your spiritual growth not just to yourself but to all humankind because we are all connected in more ways than you can imagine. The collective consciousness of all human beings in the world determines the state of the world. As of now, the world with its inequalities, hatred, violence and injustices is not exactly a pleasant place!

Now that you have come so far in this book, ask yourself whether your religion ever taught you about your seven bodies, the fallen beings, duality consciousness and the sinister force. I am sure most of you will answer 'No'. Organised religions have no desire to help you transcend your current level of consciousness—they only give false promises of a heavenly after-life. Orthodox religions offer you fixed beliefs and rules and tell you that by adhering to them, you will automatically go to heaven after death. This approach is a childish indoctrination because no outer path can ever save you. You cannot enter the spiritual realms unless you purify your consciousness; the outer path is of no use here.

Have you noticed that some people hate their own religions? In their earlier embodiments, the priesthood and religious leaders betrayed them with false promises. E.g. terrorist leaders promise heaven and a glorious afterlife to their brainwashed recruits for killing people of other religions. When these terror recruits die, they get stuck in lower emotional realms (astral hells) where they undergo tremendous suffering for their heinous actions. They feel betrayed when they realise that there are no heavenly damsels and angels to greet them. The wounds go deep, so when they re-embody, the soul remembers the past betrayal. Therefore, in the new life, they hate religion, but especially the one they followed in their earlier embodiment.

So in a nutshell, are religions good? Yes, but religion is just a baby step after which you quickly need to move on to the inner path of Christhood. Religion makes you look outside for the source of your troubles, whereas the path of Christhood will point you inwards wherein lies the cause of the problem. The inner path teaches you to take responsibility for yourself and not be dependent on some outer fictitious God.

*It takes nothing to join a crowd. It takes everything
to stand alone.*

— Hans F Hansen

CHAPTER 15
Some Experiments

Over the last several decades, some well-known psychology experiments have been conducted that give lots of insights into human nature. Many of these experiments prove that humans, generally speaking, are pliable. This is not surprising because most of humanity lives through the Unconscious-Self, which is unstable, fearful and insecure. I have briefly described three experiments.

Solomon Asch was a Polish-American gestalt psychologist and pioneer in social psychology. He conducted some interesting experiments to prove that humans relent to social pressure and conform. Both the elevator and conformity experiments were conducted by Asch.

The Elevator Experiment

This experiment involved a group of volunteers who stood inside an elevator facing the backside instead of facing the elevator door. A genuine but unsuspecting participant entered the elevator. Upon seeing the odd posture of the volunteers, he too, after a few minutes of hesitation, adopts the same posture. This behaviour is no doubt amusing, however, on the not-so-lighter note, it shows how quickly a person can perform senseless acts just because others are doing it.

The ASCH Conformity Experiment

A group of 50 students was chosen to participate in this experiment called the 'Vision Test'.

In each trial, the participants comprised eight students, one of whom was a genuine participant unaware of the objective of the experiment while the others were confederates. The confederates were in league with the experimenter and were collaborating with him to test the genuine participant.

There were 4 lines drawn on a sheet of paper. Out of the 4, one line was the target line and the participants were asked as to which of the other three lines (marked A, B, C) was equal in length to the candidate line.

Out of the 18 trials conducted, the confederates deliberately gave wrong answers in the 12 critical trials. It was found that in the critical tests at least 75% of the participants conformed and gave wrong answers in at least one trial. Overall, 32% of the participants conformed and went along with the answers given by the confederates. Another group known as the control group was formed with only genuine participants so there was no pressure to conform. In these control group trials, less than 1% of participants gave incorrect answers.

The following were the findings of the experiment:

- An individual conforms more to a group if the number of members in that group is high.

- Individuals conform more to others when the task is difficult.

- An individual conforms more to a group if the group members are of higher social standing.

- Conformity decreases if individuals are able to respond privately.

The Milgram Shock Experiment

Stanley Milgram was a psychologist at Yale University and he conducted the experiment briefly described below.

About 40 males between the age of 20 and 40 participated in this experiment. A group of two people was formed, one was the 'teacher' and the other a 'student'. The student was always a confederate or cohort of the experimenter Stanley Milgram and thus knew the purpose of the experiment. However, the teacher had no clue about anything because it was his behaviour that was the object of study. The experiment was rigged to ensure that genuine participants always got the role of teachers. There was also a person who acted as a coordinator. The student was strapped to a chair with electrodes and was given a list of word pairs by his teacher. After the student learnt the word pairs, the teacher tested him by naming a word and asking him to recall its partner word from a list of given words. If the student made a mistake, the teacher gave him an electric shock that ranged from 15 to 450 volts. As the student continued giving wrong answers, the teacher increased the level of the electric shocks. If at any point of time the teacher did not want to continue, the coordinator standing there would prod him verbally. The phrases would be 'please continue', 'the experiment requires you to continue', 'It is absolutely essential that you continue', 'you have no other choice but to continue'.

It was found that 65% of the teachers continued to give shocks to the highest level of 450 volts and all continued till 300 volts. This shows how most human beings can act cruelly upon receiving orders from a higher authority. Take note that in reality there were no electric shocks and only a recording was being played out. Nonetheless, the teachers were under the impression that the shocks were real.

The above experiments show that a) most humans have a herd mentality and will easily conform when there is social pressure b) most people act cruelly if they get such orders from a higher authority. It is now not surprising to understand why a normal person behaves like a savage when he is part of a mob. The gist of the matter is that most people have a weak sense of individuality. They are willing to throw away their individuality just to conform or obey. The above-stated experiments explain, to a large extent, why Nazi sympathisers and perpetrators supported Hitler in committing atrocities on the Jews. There are many more such examples in history.

The fallen beings, their minions and the power elite desire to control humanity and want ordinary citizens to behave like cattle. Thus, evil continues because people do not become individuals. As long as you live through your Unconscious-Self, you cannot be an individual. The personality, created by the Unconscious-Self, likes to conform and seek validation, praise and approval from others. To this end, it is willing to be servile, complaisant, unethical and even cowardly. It is only by expanding your consciousness that you can live as an authentic individual. Remember from an earlier chapter that the design pattern of every human being's electron is unique; literally, there is no one like you in all Creation. Therefore, every person must honour their uniqueness and not become a part of a herd or mob.

CHAPTER 16
Claiming Your True Identity

I assume you are now familiar with various aspects of your being: I-AM-Presence, six other bodies, Conscious-Self and the Unconscious-Self. If so, then you are ready for this chapter.

Self-actualisation is one of the most basic needs of every human being. Every person, no matter how vile, wants to become something more. No person knowingly wants to remain static. However, for most people, self-actualisation means only being driven by their Unconscious-Selves to accumulate more money and material success. Real self-actualisation is evolution, and evolution truly means growing in consciousness.

Growing in consciousness means shifting focus from your Unconscious-Self to your Conscious-Self, thereby expanding your awareness. As you move deeper into your Conscious-Self, you begin attuning with your Christ-Self and I-AM-Presence. Spiritual growth is a long process; however, once you start living through your Conscious-Self, your Christ-Self will start guiding you; you will feel its guidance when your mind is calm and your emotions harmonised. Therefore, you need not wait to reach the advanced stage of becoming one with your Christ-Self to receive guidance from it. Your Christ-Self is your only true friend in the world and wants what is best for your growth. It will never cater to your ego-driven desires. Guidance from the Christ-Self can come in the form of intuition, a feeling in the heart, the voice of conscience or a sense of knowingness.

Spiritual teachings are multifaceted so they can explain a concept in different ways. The terms 'expanding one's consciousness', 'growing spiritually', 'growing in consciousness', 'rising above duality consciousness', 'expanding one's awareness', 'moving towards enlightenment', all mean the same. However, my favourite term is 'Christ Consciousness'. To grow spiritually means to move towards your Christ-Self, thereby grow in Christ Consciousness. I want to repeat here that the word 'Christ' is a state of consciousness that every human being must endeavour to attain. It is wrong to associate this word with only Christianity.

There are 144 levels of consciousness possible on Earth; at the highest level 144, one attains full unity with their Christ-Self and becomes a 'Christ'. However, the path to Christhood is gradual, and you need to cross the levels of consciousness one at a time using spiritual techniques and insights from your life's experiences. You cannot jump from level 48 to 70 at once. When a lifestream embodies on Earth for the first time, it is at the 48th level of consciousness by default. It should ideally rise to the 144th level, but in most cases, this does not happen. The darkness on the planet drags the lifestream to levels lower than 48. The human embodies thousands of times, but at some stage it tires of all earthly experiences, such as failures, diseases, accidents and failed relationships. Now it seeks something higher—it has now reached level 48. Upon crossing level 48, the person starts manifesting degrees of Christhood.

It is very difficult to describe each level of consciousness. Still, I will give a summary (the list of qualities is not exhaustive but will give you a good idea).

Group 1 (Below 48th level)

Most people in the world (KSKMP) belong to this group. Many public figures such as politicians, celebrities and religious leaders fall into this category. The lower the level of consciousness, the more the below-mentioned traits manifest in that person.

- Entirely driven by the Unconscious-Self, so the innumerable Selves lead to a fragmented personality.

- Seek only career progress, sensuous pleasures and a comfortable life. These individuals have no awareness and interest in spiritual growth and higher realities; therefore, spiritual teachers find them unreachable.

- Very selfish and self-focused, so care only about one's own interests. Nevertheless, their self-attention becomes gleefully focused on others when finding faults with the latter. Extreme selfishness can result in sociopathy and psychopathy.

- Conviction that they can and should get away with anything. Justifying their wrong actions is a habit with such people; for them, the end justifies the means.

- Enslaved by their five senses so driven by greed and ego-driven ambition; they care for what they can take from others, not what they can give. The prime goal in life is to acquire power, money, material possessions and recognition by any means. Such people feel insecure and tensed most of the time.

- Closed mindedness and inability to listen to other people's opinions.

- Fondness for ritualistic worship that is driven by greed or fear.

- Desire to control others even by manipulation if necessary.

Group 2 (Between 48th and 96th level)

The traits mentioned in Group 1 are not present in people in this group or are in the process of dissolving. Also, the seeker begins to experience the following:

- Awareness of the Conscious-Self and the need to attune with it.

- Getting guidance from the Christ-Self which hitherto was ignored.

- Realisation that a materialistic life cannot bring permanent happiness, and only continuous spiritual growth can fulfil life's true purpose.

- Understanding that cooperation and not competition is the key to an abundant life.

- Expanded sense of awareness and feeling connected to all life on Earth; therefore, ethical behaviour comes naturally to such people.

- Increased feeling of peace and unconditional happiness.

- Understanding that the Earth is a school where lifestreams embody to learn lessons and expand their awareness.

Group 3 (Above 96th level)

The traits of people in group 1 do not exist in people in this group. The changes and experiences highlighted in group 2 become accentuated in individuals in this group. Some of the transformations that the seeker undergoes are as follows:

- Increased momentum in surrendering to the I-AM-Presence or God. Actions are now guided by the Christ-Self and not by the ego.

- The I-AM-Presence expresses itself freely through its human because the Selves blocking its way are now dissolved.

- No more reliance on outer teachers or books. Guidance comes from the I-AM-Presence through the Christ-Self and also from spiritual masters in the higher realms.

- Non-identification with one's religion, country, race and nationality. Such a person will become a universal being and will naturally harbour universal thoughts and ideas.

- Realisation that helping other individuals evolve spiritually is one of the key requirements of Christhood.

- Powers over matter may develop after crossing a certain level of consciousness. However, one must use the powers only as per guidance from the Christ-Self and not the ego.

- Awareness of the underlying unity of all Creation, thereby not feeling threatened by anyone.

- Feeling love for all life and not regarding anyone as an enemy. Of course, this does not mean ignoring the evil in this world and doing nothing about it.

At the 144th level of consciousness, all the qualities mentioned in groups 2 and 3 manifest in their full glory. Upon reaching the 144th level, one attains full Christ Consciousness and is ready to ascend (*ascension is described later in this chapter*).

Effects of an Expanding Consciousness

The levels of consciousness described above give a fairly good idea about growth in consciousness. Nonetheless, I feel tempted to describe a little more.

As you grow in Christ Consciousness, you will observe the Selves within you objectively. As your Conscious-Self starts reclaiming its energy, the Selves within you will begin to dissolve. As your screaming Selves start disappearing, you will become calmer, more peaceful and harmonious. Now you will function from the inner stillness of your Conscious-Self; thus, you will act more and react less. In other words, you will realise that you always have a choice in dealing with any situation. Therefore, you need not react because some of your Selves are mercilessly prompting you and often leading you towards adverse consequences. Remember that reaction is also an action, but actuated by your Selves, not by your Conscious-Self.

When you become centred in the blissful nothingness of your Conscious-Self, you will be easily able to adapt to any situation, change in life or uncertainty. This adaptability will arise because now the weakening Selves can no more restrict or discourage you. Remember, *the more you are nothing, the more you can be anything*! The best part about acting through the Conscious-Self is that new Selves are not created because the light from your I-AM-Presence is flowing effortlessly and doing its work. When you act through your Unconscious-Self, the Selves within you absorb the energy from your I-AM-presence and become stronger.

Your growth in Christ Consciousness will awaken your individuality and will make you an authentic and integrated person. You will get unplugged from the mass consciousness of humankind that turns individuals into herd members. You will develop Christ discernment and will no more be tempted into purchasing needless material possessions and seeking low-quality entertainment. Unlike most people, you will now look into any situation with an unbiased eye because now you are free of perception filters. Therefore, you will get a much broader insight into any situation. Besides Christ discernment, your intuitive powers will also develop and after a stage, you will sense other people's energies.

Expansion of consciousness refines the five senses and enhances creativity. Harmful habits such as smoking and alcoholism will gently leave you as because you are now vibrating at a higher rate. The higher vibrations of your body cannot tolerate anything gross or of a lower vibration. Diseases have a low vibratory rate so even a chronic illness can disappear from your body. As your sensitivity grows, you will become aware of the impact your actions and traits have on other people and vice versa.

Growth in Christhood will make you less judgmental; you will realise that every person responds to life according to their level of consciousness, so everyone's life journey is different. You will no more react with hatred or anger to someone who does not agree with you. You will start feeling one with all life, all humankind and even animals. Furthermore, you will lose the inclination to judge people based only on their worldly status and material success; you will see your fellow men as spiritual beings and not just outer personalities.

Have you ever wondered why some people are corrupt? What makes a person accept a bribe? Sure, it is greed for money, but underneath the greed is a lack of self-esteem. No truly self-respecting person will ever knowingly act unethically. Why does this lack of self-esteem arise? It is because one does not know their true identity—a glorious being of light that is none other than the individualised Creator God. When a person recognises their true identity, they cannot ever knowingly act unethically.

You already know that the sinister force and your impure four lower bodies energise the Selves within you. Additionally, your opinions, beliefs and theories also sustain your Selves. Your growth in Christ Consciousness will loosen the grip of all the concepts and holy cows that you hold dear; you will realise that they are all creations of ego-driven minds. As you rise above duality consciousness, you will leave all theories, dogmas and isms behind.

Spiritual growth brings very beneficial changes in all areas of your life; however, it will impact your psychological or mental health the most. You will become a psychologically healthy individual and attain mental freedom. Besides inner peace and harmony, some other signs of sound mental health are commitment to truth, not worrying about the past or future, not comparing oneself with others and not seeking validation from others.

Mental illness happens when a person does not have good psychological health; the myriad Selves within run amok. Tragically, humankind relates happiness with money and material possessions. There are many examples of wealthy and successful people who fell into depression and committed suicide. It is time that humankind recognises psychological health as a true measure of abundance and happiness.

The path to Christhood is very beautiful, but also very challenging. What I have highlighted above is a subset of the changes you will experience in your journey towards Christhood. It would be best if you make some discoveries yourself. 'Serendipity' is the word to remember.

Expansion Through Experience

Spiritual growth happens through techniques and also life experiences. I have explained here how it can happen through our day-to-day experiences.

Supposing, you are neutral towards animals; you neither like animals nor dislike them. One morning you open the main gate of your house only to see a very sick and hungry stray dog lying just outside the gate. The dog gives you a hopeful look and being a good person (most people have a primary degree of kindness) you take pity on the animal. You bring it inside your compound and give it food; you probably call a vet also. For several days you take care of the dog, and once it has healed you set it free. You have done this out of your basic kindness or perhaps a sense of duty—you do not have any affection for the dog. You have done a kind deed, but your consciousness has not expanded.

Now assume you developed some affection for that dog. You could see how it wagged its tail and greeted you, jumped at you in sheer delight when you came home from work and how it licked your hands and face in gratitude. Since this provides you with a portal for understanding and loving all dogs, you decide to enter the portal. Slowly but steadily your affection becomes deeper. Now you will no longer see dogs indifferently but have developed a broader understanding as to how loving these animals can be. Now your consciousness has expanded, and you have evolved. Furthermore, if your new-found love for dogs makes you love other animals as well and develop a reverence, love and understanding for them, your consciousness has expanded further—one incident has had a cascading effect.

We see from above that even our day-to-day life can contribute to our spiritual growth. However, if you are not continuously deepening attunement with your Conscious-Self by using spiritual techniques, your ability to retain insights from any experience (past or future) can be lost. In the above example, it is possible that if in future you are bitten by a dog, you may start hating dogs and perhaps other animals too. Now you have slid down in consciousness, perhaps lower than where you were before. However, if you are attuned to your Conscious-Self (thereby your Christ-Self), no future unpleasant experience will erase the insights gained from earlier similar experiences. Instead, the new experience will give you a fresh perspective and expand your awareness. So, the conclusion is that growing into Christhood only through experiences is a prolonged and unstable process. Therefore, it is imperative to use spiritual techniques to keep oneself in the radar of their Christ-Self.

A Higher Understanding of Your I-AM-Presence and Conscious-Self

In the chapter 'Your Seven Bodies', I had explained the I-AM-Presence. That was level 1 understanding to prepare you as I am sure most of you are new to this knowledge. I will now give level 2 understanding that will clear your concepts as to who you truly are.

Imagine a thick vertical tube of light called A (your I-AM-Presence) descends from above and passes through a convex lens called B (your Unconscious-Self). Upon crossing the lens, it bends and converges on the ground at a focal point called C (your Conscious-Self).

As you see from above, when A becomes localized as a small circle at a focal point, it becomes C. So the complete picture is—Your I-AM-Presence A has projected itself on Earth to create beauty, perfection and grow from its experiences. However, it encounters your Unconscious-Self B which is sustained by the impurities in your four lower bodies. The crowd of Selves that form your Unconscious-Self, significantly narrow down or reduce the light of your I-AM-Presence. Consequently, the I-AM-Presence gets reduced to a small focal point C which is your Conscious-Self.

The whole point of spiritual growth is that C now must regain its true identity, which is A, and for this, it must start dissolving the Selves that eclipse it. The more Selves C dissolves (breaking the lens B bit by bit), the more it expands. When all Selves dissolve through purification of the four lower bodies, the lens B disappears, and C fully expands and becomes one with A. The Conscious-Self now becomes one with its I-AM-Presence; this is called ascension. *Ascension is expansion.*

If you have understood and internalised the above, you are one of the very few lucky people in the world. Now you have a crystal clear understanding of what growth in Christ Consciousness is about. Now you do not need philosophies, theological texts and doctrines—they are creations of the ego-driven human mind. The path to ascension is easy to understand.

There are two things to keep in mind:

- Although your Conscious-Self is the localized emanation of your I-AM-Presence, you can regard it as a small portion of the latter.

- Ascension is the final goal and takes time; however, even as you make spiritual progress, beneficial changes start happening in your life. Even before ascending, you can be of immense service to the world.

Polishing Your Personality?

The path to Christhood is to dissolve your Unconscious-Self that is an agglomeration of thousands of Selves. Your Unconscious-Self creates your personality as a tool to interact with the world. It is vital to realise that, beyond a certain point it is a waste of time polishing your personality because eventually, you will have to give it up. It is your Conscious-Self that will ascend into higher realms, not your Unconscious-Self. Personality is a mask, so why bother trying to make the mask more beautiful when you have to give it up in any case? It is adequate if you have good manners and etiquette, are well-groomed and have socially acceptable behavioural traits. If you have some quirks, idiosyncrasies or odd habits, it is all right as long as they do not harm or inconvenience others. Instead of wasting time in overpolishing your personality, focus more on attaining higher consciousness. As your personality melts, you will become a presence and a more authentic human being who does not go around seeking validation from others.

Your I-AM-Presence Awaits Your Return

Assume you are a team manager in your workplace and have sent out one of your subordinates on an assignment to work on a project. You have given him sufficient time, but you cannot give him inordinate time. Sooner or later, you will want him back in your team and share his experiences and learning with you. Something similar happens when the Conscious-Self embodies on Earth. The I-AM-Presence gives enough time (14,000 years) to the Conscious-Self to learn from all its multiple embodiments on Earth and come back to merge with it. However, the reality is that most human beings exceed that time limit by several thousand years. Most people on Earth have remained stuck for many thousands of years and have not evolved enough to make their ascension. On Earth, human parents fret so much when their child flunks a grade and loses one year. What about the thousands of times almost every person has flunked his ascension exam?

What is Ascension?

Upon attaining full Christ Consciousness at level 144, one becomes a 'Christ'. Now all lessons on Earth are complete; the person need not embody on a dark planet like Earth again. One becomes permanently free from the discord, limitations and strife on Earth and ascends to the sixth sphere (we live in the seventh) through a process known as ascension.

When ascension happens, the Conscious-Self merges with its I-AM-Presence and becomes an ascended being or an ascended master. The consciousness of an ascended being is so vast that you can scarcely imagine. An ascended being's body is made of the pure electrons of the Creator; its beauty cannot be described in words. If an ascended being were to appear in a crowded place, every person will stop dead in their tracks for they have never seen such a beautiful being!

Ascension can happen only when the human has purified its four lower bodies (etheric, mental, emotional and physical). The purified energies are raised into the I-AM-Presence. If a human wants to ascend, it must return every ounce of energy to its I-AM-Presence that the latter had lent it for its earthly sojourn. The I-AM-Presence will take back the energy only in its pristine form.

Ascension is a total transformation of one's consciousness; it can be compared to a bud blossoming into a flower or a caterpillar transforming into a butterfly. The process of ascension continues until you reach the first sphere. If you ascend from the first sphere, you become one with the Creator Himself—this is what He wants. With every ascended being who joins Him, the Creator grows and expands—this is the purpose of all Creation. Becoming one with the Creator does not mean losing one's identity. It is like one more petal growing inside a flower or one more flower growing on a plant.

The I-AM-Presence of every lifestream is created by ascended beings. Therefore, when you ascend, you will also create I-AM-Presences and send them out to various realms to co-create, experience and learn. Every person on Earth has spiritual parents who are now ascended beings. If you have understood the picture, then you will realise how all beings in Creation connect each other—we are all cosmic siblings. There is no separation but only oneness.

Partial Ascension

During the time of Buddha and Jesus, one had to purify 100% of their energies in order to ascend. Besides, the energies of the Earth two thousand years ago were much denser than they are now. Because humankind has evolved (though not as much as it should have), the planet's energies are less dense now. In the current age, one needs to purify at least 51% of their energies in order to ascend. However, in this case, partial ascension happens. Partial ascension means that the lifestream will no longer have to embody on a dark and discord-filled planet like Earth. It will remain in the seventh sphere but will now embody on planets far more evolved and beautiful than the Earth. It is only after purifying its remaining 49% energies that the lifestream moves into the sixth sphere.

Becoming free from embodying on dark and treacherous planets like Earth is in itself a marvellous achievement. Therefore, you should not worry too much about ascending from the current sphere. Stay focused on the path of Christ Consciousness, and do not be overly concerned about tracking your spiritual progress. Be aware that it is not necessary to reach the 144th level to be free from the Earth. If you attain a sufficiently high level of consciousness, you will not have to re-embody on Earth. It would be very wise to take advantage of the 49% discount offer that the cosmic hierarchy has offered humans and shift to a more evolved planet! Move into worlds that are so beautiful that even the most scenic spot on Earth is dust compared to them.

There are billions of planets in our material universe alone and many of them are inhabited with beings more evolved than humans on Earth. Life on such planets vibrates at a much higher frequency than Earth, so it cannot be detected even by the most advanced scientific instruments in our world. Please do not give credence to the scientific community when they pontificate that Earth is the only inhabited planet in the universe. To know higher realities, you have to raise your consciousness and rise above the world of matter. Most scientists are stuck in material consciousness.

Two Ways to Live

There are two ways to live: through your Unconscious-Self (as most people do) and your Conscious-Self.

If you live through your Unconscious-Self, you will live the hard way. Tribulations, anxieties and insecurities will continuously buffet your life because of the disharmonious actions of your Unconscious-Self. Any action (good or bad) performed through the Unconscious-Self energises some existing Selves and may create new Selves. The Unconscious-Self is reactive; as a result, when a Self performs an action such as tithing, it is also a reaction—a so-called good action. Such a 'good' action does not come from the stillness of your real being (your Conscious-Self). Therefore, it carries no light and no evolutionary impulse—it is just an action that is mechanically performed. Often, praise or publicity-seeking Selves motivate the so-called good actions. You already know that to grow in Christ Consciousness, you will have to dissolve all your Selves, including the 'good' ones. Goodness cannot be a habit but has to come from your presence, not your personality. However, till the time one achieves a certain degree of alignment with their Conscious-Self, they should perform only 'good' actions.

When you act from your Conscious-Self, you act from the stillness of your inner being. You will not be trapped in the duality of 'good' and 'bad' action; your action will flow like a river. Your actions will be imbued with love and harmony because now it is your I-AM-Presence expressing itself freely through your Conscious-Self. There are no screaming Selves to block the light from your I-AM-Presence. The more you act from your Conscious-Self, the lesser karma you create for yourself. No action that is guided by the Christ-Self can ever be wrong. Remember, the I-AM-Presence created the physical body to create beauty and harmony on Earth, so it does not expect to be disturbed by the howling Selves.

There is only one failure in life—not having grown in consciousness from youth to old age. If you do not grow in Christ Consciousness and remain the same person all your life, you truly miss an opportunity. Your wealth, power, status and knowledge have no meaning if they do not actuate you to expand your consciousness. True, you will build up a karmic momentum of earning material success and wealth. This momentum will help you in your future embodiments; however, it will trap you further in a karmic cycle and prevent you from ascending to higher realms. This cycle can go on for thousands of embodiments; that is why it is known as the wheel of 'Samsara'. Your consciousness, not your material possessions and worldly success, is your reality. Therefore, it is profoundly wise to improve the quality of your consciousness. Walk the path of Christ Consciousness because spending your life without having known your real self is a very unwise way to live.

A Higher Explanation of Karma

Any action performed through the Unconscious-Self creates karma. If the Unconscious-Self is a blackboard, then any action performed through it adds a scribble on the blackboard. On the other hand, the Conscious-Self is formless and emptiness so any action from it leaves no trace of karma. To reach the point of full ascension, you must balance or erase all your karmas. If your karmic blackboard has too many scribbles, it will take you long to wipe it clean. A person's destiny is determined by the karmas, memories and impressions stored in their four lower bodies. Purification of these bodies is imperative to change one's destiny.

Eastern religions have given karma a very fatalistic face. According to them if once you make a mistake or commit an evil act, there is no way you can escape the consequences. In a sense, this is true because whatever you do in life has consequences. Nevertheless, this is an incomplete picture of the law of karma. Whenever you act, you send out a karmic impulse into the four levels of the universe. If you have not transcended the consciousness that sent out that impulse, then you will undoubtedly reap the consequences of that action. On the other hand, if you have risen above the earlier state of consciousness, the returning impulse will not affect you; it will get dissolved in the etheric, mental or emotional realms. Even if it does reach the physical realm, it will have become weak and have minimal effect on you. The returning impulse can happen in the same life or some future lifetime—there is no fixed rule about this. The example in the paragraph below will give greater clarity on this concept.

Suppose a man named A, murders another man named B. Going by the karmic law, this action will lead to consequences such as A getting murdered or dying a premature death in an accident in the same lifetime or some future embodiment. Supposing, after ten years, the returning karmic impulse starts its journey back to A. However, during these ten years, A has realised his mistake and transcended his earlier state of consciousness. Now the returning karmic impulse will get dissipated in the three realms before entering the physical realm. Even if the returning impulse does strike

A, it will result in a minor injury or illness. However, if A has remained the same person and is not contrite, he is likely to die a violent death as a 'punishment' for murdering B. A key point to note is that for A to transcend his level of 'murderer' consciousness, he would have to completely dissolve all the Selves that incite him into killing another human being; this is not easy and requires spiritual techniques. The change should happen at the most fundamental level of one's being; simply imagining that one has changed is not enough.

The universe wants to teach you and help you evolve; it has no desire to punish you, no matter what organised religions and priests say. Often, a person experiences delayed results of their evil karma because the universe gives them time to rectify their errors. No matter what mistake a person has made, they can always transcend that mistake by permanently raising their consciousness higher than the level of consciousness that actuated the inharmonious action. Furthermore, one can erase their karma by invoking a high-frequency light *(discussed in chapter 18)* and thus escape the consequences of their discordant actions. However, besides using this light, they should endeavour to grow in consciousness. If one does not reform but continues to use this technique to erase their evil actions, it will eventually backfire on them—sacred energies should not be misused.

Organised religions offer shortcuts, such as performing rituals, donating money and embracing redemptive suffering to escape the consequences of evil karma. None of these shortcuts ever work! The universe will not let you escape unless you have learnt your lesson by transforming your consciousness. Even when bad karma returns with terrible consequences, the universe intends to teach you that if you do not change, ordeals will continue manifesting in your life.

It is vital to know that the law of karma is impersonal; it is like a mirror and reflects your thoughts and actions. The word 'karma' simply means action; the consequences of the action depend upon your intent. If you intend to experience fortunate events in your life, you must perform harmonious actions before the karmic mirror. Likewise, if you frown or make angry faces, it will reflect unpleasant experiences. You should treat all actions you perform in life as experiments—life itself is an experiment. Putting your finger in a candle flame and hurting yourself is also an experiment. The flame is not to blame because it holds no grudge against you. It is a process that if you play with fire without taking precautions, you will burn yourself. It is worth knowing that the spiritual teachers in the higher realms do not condemn any person because of the latter's karma. They see our actions as experiments and desire that we conduct experiments intelligently so as not to reap harmful consequences. Despite what orthodox religions say, there is no judgmental God in the skies to assess our karma and then label us as 'good' or 'bad' person.

Humankind creates negative karma in thousands of ways, and one of the worst karmas is to impose upon someone's free will by dominating them. It creates a severe karmic debt with the person who gets dominated. Be careful that you do not dominate others because it creates a karmic debt and almost always leads to suppressed emotions in the person you dominate. Suppressed emotions of anger and resentment can lead to cancer.

Krishna consciousness is the same as Christ Consciousness—the word 'Krishna' is like 'Christna'. 'Vasudeva' (Lord Krishna) and 'Jesus' were individuals who attained this consciousness and so are titled 'Krishna' and 'Christ' respectively.

CHAPTER 17
Purifying & Protecting Yourself

Humans suffer due to many reasons. We have already seen how the sinister force unleashes miseries and ordeals on humans.

There are six ways in which suffering enters a person's life:

- Every negative thought, in proportion to its intensity, boomerangs on the person who releases it. The universe is the perfect mathematician and holds every human being accountable for even the tiniest bit of energy they misqualify. All toxic energies released by evil and discordant thoughts go back to the person releasing those thoughts. The returning energies cause diseases, depression, failure in career and relationships, accidents and other adversities.

- As with negative thoughts, physical actions intended to harm others also boomerang on the perpetrator. Actions such as dominating, cheating, manipulating, inflicting violence and bad-mouthing will inevitably bring adverse consequences on the perpetrator. Negative karma from previous embodiments is stored in the four lower bodies and springs up at the opportune time and causes distress in the person's life.

- Negativity directed by others through strong thoughts and words of anger, jealousy, violence and criticism. Psychic attacks, curses and black magic can also cause immense harm. Thoughts are things, and another person's strong negative thoughts will undoubtedly adversely affect you unless you keep yourself protected. Cruel words from other people can lead to depression. However, as stated above, the attacks directed at you will boomerang on the sender too.

- Toxic energies released by violence in society (wars, terrorism, communal riots and racial killings) adversely affect the energy field of human beings. At an individual level, a disturbed energy field can lead to diseases, psychological problems and other tribulations. The mass consciousness of humankind comprises harmful energies released by individuals through impure thoughts. During wars and riots, humans release tremendous hatred and anger, thereby amplifying these dark energies. Just as an oil spill spreads to other parts of the sea, potent toxic energies released by humans spread and harm people in other parts of the world.

- Discarnates attach themselves to the person and cause depression; diseases; rage; accidents; loss in career, relations and business.

- Every person is connected to other people, places and events from both their current and previous embodiments through invisible energy lines. These energy lines keep every person on Earth chained to the dense vibrations of the planet. Only after becoming an ascended being will you be able to see these energy lines; they will appear like the lines of light of a city as seen from space. These energy lines or cords send out impulses that can be a source of energy drain and tribulations in a person's life. Often, unpleasant incidents happen in a person's life that was unnecessary but occurred because the energy lines triggered them.

How can you protect yourself from all tribulations caused by the above? I want to introduce you to the 'violet flame'—the most potent technique of spiritual protection available on Earth.

The violet flame is a high-frequency energy that negative energies cannot catch up with. Invoking the violet flame increases the spinning speed of the electrons in the body, thereby protecting the body from the lower frequencies of diseases, accidents, depression and so forth. The violet flame transmutes only the negative, never anything positive. If you invoke the violet flame daily, depression will not touch you. This sacred flame also erases the energy lines mentioned above.

Upon invoking the violet flame, it does the following: transmutes the negative thought-forms from the energy field, erases bad karma from current and previous embodiments and cleans the aura. As a result, the effects of the above-stated causes do not manifest in the individual's life. Just as water washes the physical body, the violet flame cleans not only the physical but also the etheric, mental and emotional bodies. Many unpleasant memories stored in the etheric body need to be erased, or else they continue to cause distress in the individual's life without the person even being aware of them. The violet flame erases the cause and effect of these memories. One must use the violet flame regularly and religiously.

THE TECHNIQUE - You could be seated on a chair or even be standing while doing this technique. Intensely imagine a violet coloured fire surging through every cell, electron, organ and gland within your body. This will remove toxins, impurities, and negative energies from your physical body. Now extend your imagination of the violet fire outside your physical body. Visualise it surrounding your physical body (above your head also) in a circular pillar-like shape till a distance of three feet—the emotional, mental and etheric bodies are bigger than the physical body. The violet fire will purge your etheric, emotional and mental bodies of negative energies, entities (spirits of disembodied humans) and harmful thought-forms attached to your aura. In case you find it difficult to visualise the violet fire simultaneously both within and outside your physical body, you can first focus within your physical body and then outside it or vice versa. You can even visualise the violet flame cleaning not only your seven chakras but also the organs of your body, such as kidneys, lungs and liver. You should invoke the violet flame for at least ten minutes daily, and if you do this more than once a day, it is even better. Remember, the more intensely you invoke the violet fire, the faster you get the benefits. As the toxic energies in your energy field are purified, you will be able to lift yourself out of the miasma of negative energies that envelope this planet. Most people spend their entire lives submerged in the toxic ocean of dense planetary energies and are never able to realise their real purpose in life.

As you continue with the violet fire technique, you will increasingly feel light, happy, healthy and clear-headed. In fact, within a week of invoking the violet flame, you will notice a difference in your being. Your aura will become cleaner and more robust. One of the most profound effects of the violet fire is that it enhances your creativity. This sacred flame will also slow down the ageing of your physical body. To encourage yourself in your violet flame practice, always be mindful that violet flame cannot be defeated by lower energies.

Take note that the violet flame does a deep cleaning of the four lower bodies and you might experience (this may not happen to everyone) old memories resurfacing. Consequently, you might enter a temporary phase of mood swings, irritability, anger and other negative feelings; this is a good sign that the flame is working on you, and you should not stop invoking the violet fire.

The violet flame works similar to a dredging machine that first brings up all the filth lying at the bottom of the pond to the surface. The action of the machine disturbs and muddies the water in the pond. However, this is a temporary phenomenon; after a while, the mud settles and the pond becomes clean. If you do not experience the reawakening of painful memories, do not assume that the violet flame is not working—it works for everyone. It is doing its job and you should invoke it forever. This sacred flame will save you from a lot of trouble in life.

A vital thing to keep in mind is that you should never abuse or misuse this sacred flame. Undoubtedly the violet flame, if invoked with sufficient intensity and duration, will clear your bad karma. However, this does not mean that you continue to perform wrong actions and keep invoking this flame to clear their affects—if you do this, someday it will backfire on you and your spiritual growth will stop. Do not be like the person who commits discordant actions and then goes to the church every time to make confessions. You must sincerely endeavour to become a better person, evolve and grow spiritually. Never take sacred energies for granted.

CHAPTER 18
Some More Techniques

The journey towards Christhood is a process and requires practising some specific techniques. Unless you diligently practise the techniques, you cannot grow in Christ Consciousness. These techniques aim at purifying the four lower bodies, healing psychological wounds and protecting oneself. Your spiritual practices will enable you to attune to your Conscious-Self by dissolving your Selves and also erase or balance your karma. There are also some dos and don'ts that, if adhered to, will speed up your progress. The violet flame is very, very useful for purifying and protecting the lower bodies and also healing psychological wounds. However, if needed, one can go in for therapy for resolving psychological issues.

Even the most sublime spiritual teachings and techniques can turn into religion and become mechanical. Many spiritual students cannot make any progress because they focus too much on the techniques and forget the reason they are practising them. Whatever techniques you follow, practice them, as far as possible, from the inner core of your being—your authentic self. Do not turn them into a ritual or a mechanical habit. On days when you are ill, do not feel compelled to practice them. However, it would be best if you practised them as regularly as you can, especially the violet flame.

If you use the techniques with sincerity, you will ascend the various levels of consciousness and your identity will start to change. You will shift from your false identity (Unconscious-Self) to your lower true identity (Conscious-Self), then to your Christ identity (Christ-Self) and then to your highest true identity (I-AM-Presence). Note that upon attaining your Christ identity, you will also attain your highest true identity.

Concentrating upon either your I-AM-Presence or Christ-Self takes you closer to the other. As a general rule, when you want to concentrate, then focus on your I-AM-Presence. When you seek guidance on any matter or have a material need, you should talk to your Christ-Self. However, there is no rigid rule so you can pray and/or focus on either one.

After a certain stage in your spiritual journey you will wonder how you have been living so long through your false identity.

Purifying the Four Lower Bodies

The four lower bodies interpenetrate each other. The emotional body is the largest and covers the mental, etheric and the physical body.

Mental body - This body should be free from worries; distress; pictures of imperfection for oneself, others or for any situation. The mental body should also be free from the burden of outdated concepts and knowledge, and should remain fresh and ready for new knowledge.

Emotional body - Purification of this body will free it from negative emotions: anger, fear and hatred, to name a few. When negativity disappears from this body then enthusiasm for life, lightness of spirit and hope appear.

Etheric body - When this body is purified, all memories of past injustices and betrayals, resentments and hurts, failures in any endeavour are released. When dark memories get purged from your etheric self, you will realise you are a divine being in a physical body.

Physical body - A purified physical body leads to vibrant health, prolonged life because of slower ageing and less need for sleep.

It is vital to remember that diseases first manifest in the etheric body. Next, they manifest in the mental body and then the emotional. The physical body is the last stage and in this body it becomes challenging to cure a disease. The other three bodies are not as dense as the physical body. Therefore, if the violet flame dissolves the disease matrix from the etheric, mental and emotional bodies, the disease will not manifest in the physical body. Often, diseases such as cancer relapse because the impure energy of the disease is still lurking in the other three lower bodies.

Here are some techniques; you should practice them for at least ten minutes. It is not necessary to do all of them on the same day.

Invoking Light

Channelling light from your I-AM-Presence is an essential technique for spiritual growth. In reality, light from your I-AM-Presence flows into your body by entering the heart, and from there it spreads out to other areas of your body; this is how your I-AM-Presence sustains life inside you. When you practise the technique, the flow of light becomes more potent.

Your I-AM-Presence is continuously seeking to send more light to our dark planet; it wants you to become an open door for this light. This light is spiritual and of a very high frequency, so beyond the range of human vision. Nonetheless, as you invoke more of this light, you will start feeling it—you must endeavour to become an electrode for this light. Whenever you have free time, imagine the light from your I-AM-Presence flowing through you.

Before I describe the benefits, here is the technique:

Sit on a chair and make sure you are alone and undisturbed. Feel your I-AM-Presence approx 12 feet above your head as a brilliantly shining golden body similar to your physical body but bigger. You can also imagine your I-AM-Presence as a big luminous mass or ball of light emanating love and light.

Now imagine and feel a steady stream of white light flowing from your I-AM-Presence into your heart. Imagine this glorious light spreading from your heart to all over your body, including your brain. Feel this light entering every organ and all the cells of your body. Keep doing this for about ten minutes. You can also imagine the white light surrounding and engulfing you in tremendous love.

Benefits of invoking light from your Presence

a)   Every time you focus on your I-AM-Presence, a cylindrical tube of light starts to form around you as protection. This tube of light protects you from all the negativity and discord (the sinister force) that is all around you. The more you practice this technique, the stronger this tube of light becomes. Take note that *your* inharmonious feelings and thoughts can create cracks in this pillar; for continued protection, you must maintain harmony in your feelings.

b)   When the light from your I-AM-Presence enters your body, it nourishes the cells and this has benefits such as slowing down ageing, more energy and less need for sleep. Always remember that this light sustains you every second of your life—you are a being of light. Your flesh body is just a garment that your Conscious-Self wears to experience the physical plane. Drawing light from your I-AM-Presence will benefit you in many ways. You will gradually start experiencing beneficial changes in your life. The more light you retain inside your body, the better your life will be in all aspects.

c) One of the most potent benefits of drawing light from your I-AM-Presence is a feeling of wholeness. Upon regular practice, after sufficient light accumulates within your body, you will experience wholeness as never before. Most people do not know what wholeness is, yet it is precisely what they crave at a deeper level. Experiencing wholeness is feeling one's entire being as a harmonious whole.

Let me explain this a little more.

Have you wondered why most people run after money, fame and material possessions? Not that these things in themselves provide contentment and happiness, but it is the FEELING that these things produce that provide satisfaction and so-called happiness. I call it so-called happiness because the happiness obtained from material possessions is merely a sensation that pleases the five senses for a while and then disappears. Ask yourself whether the car you purchased some years ago still makes you happy or do you want a new one now? Genuine happiness comes from mental freedom and is always unconditional—it is an inner feeling that does not depend on anything outside you. Humans are seeking wholeness, and most people wrongly think that material possessions and worldly success provide wholeness.

As you continue to draw light from your I-AM-Presence, you will realise that true wholeness does not depend on anything outside of you: worldly success, material possessions and status. As the light from your I-AM-Presence begins to accumulate inside your body, you will, perhaps for the first time in your life, know true happiness and contentment. As you progress, you will increasingly feel happy for no reason, and this is one of the best signs of spiritual progress. Now you know that your real being is bliss and needs nothing on the outside to feel happy. You will realise that you are in this world to spread the light of your I-AM-Presence.

<u>Channelling light for healing the world, etc.</u>

You can extend the above technique of drawing light from your I-AM-Presence also to heal the world. When you step into an unlit room and switch on the light, immediately the darkness disappears. So what is darkness? It is merely the absence of light, not the opposite of light. The evil in this world is dark, and when light enters darkness disappears.

Draw the light from your I-AM-Presence as described above and fill your entire body with light. Now imagine and feel strongly the light moving outside your body and spreading into the world. You can send the light anywhere you want, such as your home, neighbourhood, city, country, workplace, areas of violent conflicts. Remember, our planet is full of dense and negative energies—it is a dark realm. Channeling light enables high-frequency light from the spiritual realms to enter the Earth's atmosphere and eradicate darkness.

If a critical mass of people invokes light regularly, a lot of positive changes will happen in the world. Some changes would be corruption getting exposed, lessening of violent conflicts, fallen beings permanently removed from the Earth, Nature getting healed, and more. The invoking of the violet flame and the light from the I-AM-Presence by a critical mass of people will raise the frequency of the entire planet and change the Earth.

Desolidifying Technique

This technique will make your consciousness more fluid. We see solid objects, such as our gadgets and furniture, around us all the time. This 'solidifies' our consciousness and makes us believe in the solidity of Creation and that nothing can be changed—things are the way they are. Nothing in Creation is solid because the Creator's energy (Universal-Light-Substance) builds all forms. Your laptop and computer table are both made from the same energy that is vibrating differently in the two objects. All that we humans perceive as solid comprises electrons—the building blocks of life.

This technique first needs to be done with inanimate objects, so make sure there are no people or pets around. Sit comfortably and be relaxed. Focus on any object such as your computer, chair or table. Make sure you do not label it—only see the object. Now feel the energy that is making the innumerable electrons beneath the solid surface spin at terrific speeds around their nuclei. Do this for several minutes or as long as you can. As you progress in this technique, you can focus on multiple objects; in the beginning, however, it is best to use a single item. When you persist with this technique, you will start noticing that your mind is getting freed from something but do not bother to analyse it. You can practice this technique as often as you like, and as you progress you can practice it even on humans and animals.

No civilisation can progress without languages, so we humans label all animate and inanimate forms—these labels are just words and nothing more. A rose does not ask you to call it a 'Rose'. The rose is what it is—a formation of electrons. When you look at objects without labelling them and feel the electrons and the energy behind them, it will make your consciousness fluid. You will start realising that you can overcome any adverse situation, and a rigid view of life is unnecessary.

Observing Silence

Sitting alone in silence is essential. However, some people find it challenging to be alone. One reason could be they are insecure people. An insecure person usually cannot stay alone and is almost always in the company of other people, such as family members, relatives and friends. If left alone, they get busy with their gadgets, social media and other distractions. You need total self-honesty in ascertaining whether you are an insecure person. Once you become aware, this is the first step; you should get into the habit of spending some time alone every day. You must realise that it is not wise to give the bulk of your time to the world. If you realise this in old age, it might be too late. Once you have become accustomed to staying alone, you can take up the techniques below.

There are many variations to the technique of sitting in silence. For all of the below, sit alone in a place where you are not disturbed. Sit in a comfortable posture and keep your eyes closed. You can practice the techniques for ten minutes or longer if you wish.

- Focus on your I-AM-Presence that stands 12 to 50 feet above your physical body—you need not draw the light. Just feel the love of your Presence inside and outside of you. Feel its life and energy throbbing inside your body. As you continue to focus on your I-AM-Presence, you will begin to merge with it.

- Focus on the profound silence that is beneath all the physical structures inside your body. You need to do this for the entire body together and feel the inner silence that spreads throughout your body. Feeling the silence within will make you feel a whole and complete person; you will no longer feel fragmented.

- Observe the thoughts that are floating about in your mind. Just watch them and do not resist any thought, no matter how disturbing it is. The more you resist, the more it will persist just like any misfortune. When you persist in this technique, you will no longer identify with your thoughts. The Unconscious-Self of most individuals mercilessly controls the human. Most people feel alive only because of the continuous stream of thoughts generated by their Unconscious-Selves. Humanity has very little awareness of the profound and blissful silence of the Conscious-Self.

- Imagine that you are in space and watching the planet Earth. Feel strongly that you are leaving the Earth behind because all your lessons there are now complete and you are moving into higher realms. This technique can help when you are burdened with many worries and anxieties.

- You know by now that all Creation is energy vibrating at different rates, and there is nothing solid in Creation, at least not in the way we humans perceive. Everything that appears solid is, in reality, made of countless electrons vibrating at tremendous speeds. There is nothing physical that separates you from the higher realms. With your eyes closed imagine you are flying at great speed and crossing the gates of the seven spheres one by one and merging into the Creator, a great ball of white light.

- Imagine that you are spreading all across your locality, then your city and country. Keep stretching your imagination further and feel you are spreading all across the Earth. Keep going and now extend your imagination all across the universe. This exercise will help your mind to attune to vastness. Your real nature is infinite because your I-AM-Presence has a consciousness so vast that as an unascended human, you cannot comprehend it.

Some Dos and Don'ts

- Do not judge others, but look at your faults and weed them out one by one. Judging others is very enticing because it makes you feel superior, but it also traps you in a karmic spiral with the person you judge. However, you have the freedom to state a fact without feeling superior; this way you are not being judgmental. Take caution, that even while stating a fact, you do not generate anger or hatred or else you create karma for yourself and pollute your four lower bodies. Facts should be stated objectively and with a high motive, such as making any situation or person better, choosing the right course of action and endeavouring to find the truth in any matter.

- As you make progress towards Christ Consciousness your Unconscious-Self will try its best to divert you from the path. It will use the Selves within you, that are created from your political and religious beliefs, as hooks. You might experience anger, resentment, irritability and restlessness in certain situations (especially those that disturb your cherished beliefs), but this is a temporary phase. The key thing is to remain ever vigilant against dark thoughts.

- Whatever you give attention to, both pleasant and unpleasant, multiplies or expands in your life. Therefore, it is not wise to focus on negative news and tragic events. Millions of people pour their fear, anger and worries into the Earth's atmosphere, thereby precipitating more such events. This is the reason that when the media highlights an unpleasant event that becomes big news, more such incidents occur. It is all right to discuss an adverse event provided you do it objectively without getting emotionally involved.

- Do not place too much hope or expectations in human relationships. Till the time a person has reached 96th or higher level of consciousness, their conduct will be unreliable. Most of us have been through situations where a person's attitude has completely surprised us. Most relationships are driven by the Unconscious-Selves of the people and lack depth. It is best to focus on your spiritual growth and cultivate a relationship with your I-AM-Presence.

- Never try to impose, curtail or control someone's free will as this is one of the worst actions one can perform—it also creates a severe karmic debt with the dominated person. Advise only when asked but do not, under any circumstances, force the other person to change. Every human being is at a certain level of consciousness; they will transform into something higher only upon seeing a higher example or reference point. You can be that higher reference point but do not force change upon that person even if you think you are doing it for their good. Every person progresses at their own pace.

- As far as possible, do not take things personally. If someone hurts your feelings, remember that only a few of their Selves have known a few of your Selves and vice versa. Neither of you fully know the other person, and if you did, there would be total harmony between you two.

- Forgiving your enemy does not mean hugging them, befriending them and inviting them for dinner. It simply means not to harbour any ill-will towards them, not think about them and not give them energy through your attention. Forgiveness means to release your enemies from your consciousness. If someone has harmed you out of any mala fide intent, they will surely reap the consequences. You are under no obligation to be warm and friendly towards everyone just because you are spiritual person. Be alert and do not allow anyone to manipulate you.

- Please maintain a balance in whatever techniques you practice (violet flame, unfed flame, channelling light from your I-AM-Presence, etc.). Do not practice so much that you ignore your family, job and worldly duties. Lastly, remember that all techniques deliver results, but it is a gradual process, so do not expect immediate results—this is not instant coffee.

The Violet flame

CHAPTER 19
Electrons, the Body of God

Electrons are the building blocks of Creation, so everything that happens in our world is actually an electronic event. You might have read about electrons from the scientific perspective. In reality, electrons are much more than science stuff; they are the very body of God or the Creator. When the Creator began to create, He did so by emitting His Light—this light is present in everything in Creation.

The Creator's light is the pure Universal-Light-Substance (referred to as ULS in the remaining chapter) and is present in every nook and corner of Creation. Everything we see around us, such as our bodies, planets, furniture, gadgets and automobiles, is made from the ULS. The electrons in the ULS are always spinning around, so nothing in Creation is dead, and even the so-called inanimate objects are alive and pulsate the breath of God. The ULS consists of intelligent and conscious electrons that respond to the creative power of higher intelligence, such as humans and ascended beings. When a person wants to create something, they first think and come up with an idea. Then they imagine the idea and charge it with emotions. The emotionally charged thought gets impinged on the omnipresent ULS that obediently takes the shape of what the human wants to create. This is how manifestation takes place—you are free to create any experience you want with the ULS.

From the above, we see that if Creation is a painting then the ULS is the canvas. The ULS is conscious but not self-aware. However, just as millions of bricks make up a building, individual conscious units of the ULS when combined, become something much higher that vibrates at a greater speed—a self-aware entity called a human being. The electrons in the human body are spinning at a much higher speed than those present in a table. Therefore, a human being is more evolved than a table. Creation is units of ULS interacting with one another. The more evolved units act upon and influence the less evolved units. The process is the same in all spheres in Creation.

The ULS in its most basic form is malleable like Plaster of Paris and will make any form (beautiful or ugly) according to the thought-blueprint imposed upon it by a higher intelligence. Under the influence of the fallen consciousness and the sinister force, humankind mostly creates negative thought-forms that get impinged on the ULS. This misuse of the ULS creates ugly manifestations in the form of wars, violence, pollution, diseases and natural disasters. Nevertheless, the ULS has a built-in safety mechanism—it ultimately dissolves anything created from anti-Christ or duality consciousness. We know from history that evil dictatorships, corrupt Governments and depraved civilisations always collapse and disappear—there are many such examples. Though evil is ultimately self-destructive, it does not mean that humanity should ignore it and do nothing to eradicate it. Every form of life, be it individual or collective such as a society or civilisation, in Creation, can evolve, devolve or remain static. If it devolves or remains static, it will ultimately collapse and disappear.

The I-AM-Presence of every human being sends billions of intelligent electrons every second to the physical body in rhythmic pulsation. The electrons flow down like a beautiful stream of billions of beads of light to the Christ-Self and then to the physical body which they enter through the heart. These electrons in their pure state are full of vitality and power—they also contain the blueprint for the fulfilment of the divine plan for that person. Nonetheless, upon entering the human body, they become contaminated by the impurities in the four lower bodies and get buffeted and coloured by dark and inharmonious thoughts and feelings. When the muddied electrons get impinged upon the ULS, unfortunate incidents happen in the person's life. Thus, the collected impure thoughts of human beings have created ugly forms such as poverty, terrorism and environmental destruction all over the world.

The electrons sent to you by your I-AM-Presence is the priceless raw material that you should utilise to create beauty and harmony in the world. The more creatively you use your electrons, the more of these electrons will be sent to you by your I-AM-Presence—this is how you multiply your talents. Have you observed that many professionals, especially in creative fields, lose their touch after achieving success and fame? Their complacency and arrogance reduce the flow of electrons, so their outputs become mediocre. If only such individuals realised that their I-AM-Presence is the source of everything and can supply them with endless talent! It is a pity that humankind misuses their God-gifted electronic raw material to such a great extent. It is vital to maintain emotional harmony so that these electronic workers sent by the I-AM-Presence can quietly go about doing their work of manifesting beauty and happiness in one's life. Maintaining emotional harmony necessitates purification of the four lower bodies.

Electrons and the Physical Body

All four lower bodies are made of electrons that are constantly spinning; in their natural state, the electrons are pure and spin at the right speed. However, inharmonious feelings and negative emotions accumulate upon the electrons, thereby making them heavy. Consequently, their spinning speed slows down and the electrons get thrown off from their natural orbits. The disturbance caused to the electrons leads to premature ageing, diseases, ailments and other bodily imperfections. Note that children and youngsters have glowing skin and bright faces that reflect purity. Nevertheless, with age most people start accumulating the discord of the world in their four lower bodies. Therefore, after the age of thirty, in most people, the skin starts losing its glow and other imperfections begin to manifest on the body. You might have noticed that in some people, the skin becomes darker with age.

Among all the four bodies, the emotional body has the maximum impact on the physical appearance and health of a person. It is essential to use the violet flame every day without fail to maintain harmony in emotions. Besides invoking the violet flame, you should also expand the threefold unfed flame in your heart. This technique will increase the vibratory rate of your four lower bodies and dislodge the discord accumulated on their electrons. Your human structure is a garment of billions and billions of electrons that are pure beings of light and are just waiting to bring perfection into your life. Invoking the violet flame and expanding the unfed flame are the right methods to bring your physical body to a state of beauty and health. Please remember that whatever technique you use, you must maintain harmony in emotions.

Every human being radiates energy known as personal magnetism. This energy comprises the electrons that are continuously leaving your body and touching every living being and inanimate object that you come in contact with. Therefore, you should avoid eating food cooked by an angry person or someone who harbours adverse feelings for you. The food gets contaminated by the electrons charged with hostile feelings emanated by the person cooking the food. You can, however, purify the food by visualising it within the violet flame. It is possible that in future, fingerprinting will become obsolete because technology will detect the electrons left behind by criminals.

It would be wise not to view life superficially but feel the underlying forces behind all phenomena including the processes taking place within our bodies.

Electronic View of Life

It is time for humanity to adopt an electronic view of life. People get so attached to their material possessions. Have you ever deeply thought, what is a diamond? It is a temporary matrix of electrons that appears to the sense of sight in a shape and size that we humans call 'Diamond'. Ditto is the case with every object around us. When you begin to see everything around you as a matrix of electrons, your consciousness will start becoming free. Material possessions will start losing their grip on you. No more will window-shopping in a trendy mall tempt you to enter the shop and purchase something you do not need. This freedom is very experiential, and words cannot fully describe it.

The stream of electrons from the I-AM-Presence is of a much higher vibration than the ULS that is present outside the human body and spread all over Creation.

CHAPTER 20
Fighting Life?

Having come this far, you now have a good idea of what is life all about. You are the Creator individualised who has descended into the physical universe to make the world beautiful, learn from its experiences and ascend into the spiritual realms to continue its evolution from there—it is as simple as that.

Your ego is exceptionally cunning and will never give up on its efforts to mislead you and keep you trapped in matter consciousness. As you grow into Christ Consciousness, your ego will start to dissolve. Your spiritual progress is a direct threat to your ego, and it will struggle with its full strength to prevent you from expanding your consciousness. There are millions of ways your ego can mislead you, but there is one trick it plays that works on most people—epic tales of struggle.

Many people succeed in their material life after going through a lot of difficulties, poverty and struggles. You too could be one such person. We often read or hear about the stories of such people and narrate these stories to our children to inspire them. The critical point to note here is that what appears inspiring is not always so. These stories of struggles against odds have caused most people to assume that life is innately unfair, life is to be fought with and struggled against, time is money and so on. If you have read the chapter on electrons, you know that thoughts generated by human beings influence the Universal-Light-Substance. When humans give emotional energy to struggles, difficulties and 'fight with life' scenarios, the Universal-Light-Substance creates such forms and events that actually make life a struggle. It is unwise to give too much importance to stories of struggle. Remember, words are powerful, and when a phrase becomes popular through media (print, social and electronic) and public figures, it starts influencing the subconscious minds of people. Catchy slogans incite people for wars and riots. Most people are at a low level of consciousness, so they get easily influenced by these slogans—millions have died because of words alone.

It is a strange truth that many people subconsciously love problems and difficulties because surmounting them boosts their egos. Therefore, they attract such situations in their lives. Other reasons for difficult situations in life are bad karma created in current and previous embodiments and impurities in the four lower bodies. A person takes birth in a low-income family or a particular country because of karmic reasons. In a nutshell, the afflictions a person faces in their life are a result of their own doing. Given this logic, it makes no sense for you to emotionally absorb the struggle stories of other people (especially celebrities and other public figures) and make them your stories. Nevertheless, it is all right to objectively glean some practical learning from such stories as this can help you. Your life's computer should have files that you create; do not download life-files of other people no matter how famous they are.

Every person's life journey is different; someone else's journey should not be your journey. Now that you know about your I-AM-Presence and the violet flame, you should use these techniques to transmute your negative energies and erase your bad karma. If you imagine your physical body to be a pipe then your bad karma, impure thoughts and misqualified energies are like the sludge that prevents the light from your I-AM-Presence flowing through—this is the reason for all your struggles and problems. Remove the sludge and the light will flow through unhindered and do its work. The light from your I-AM-Presence is the light of the Creator and has no opposites. The techniques suggested in this book, if practised, will save you from a lot of troubles, struggles and many 'fight with life' episodes.

Children are very impressionable so take extra care not to relate such stories (do not glorify even *your* struggles) to them, lest from childhood they become conditioned to think that fighting with life is the only way to live. Why give energy to struggles when all they do is delay your accomplishments and give you pain? Everyone faces difficult situations in life and should learn from them; however, your struggles should be your own, not someone else's. There is nothing heroic about facing unnecessary problems in your life. Watch out, for your ego will delude you in many ways and make you feel like a hero. Observe Nature and see how flowers blossom effortlessly. The light from your I-AM-Presence, when allowed to flow unhindered, does everything according to the divine plan and creates beauty and joy.

CHAPTER 21
Defeating Evil

Having gained knowledge about duality consciousness and fallen beings, you now know that every aspect of life is affected by the fallen consciousness.

The Creator has given free will to all humans; this free will is total and unconditional. The Earth is a school for human beings to create, learn and grow from their experiences. For this reason, the gift of free will is indispensable; if something external controls humans, they cannot experiment and learn. Humans are free to experiment with their free will and even perform evil actions, just as the fallen beings did in their earlier spheres. However, evil actions always have unpleasant outcomes. No lifestream can ever escape the consequences of their inharmonious thoughts and actions. Very often, the results of evil deeds throw the perpetrator into a reactive spiral, and this sows the seeds of more evil. In conclusion, it is the misuse of free will, a gift from the Creator, which creates so much evil in the world.

For defeating evil, the very first step is to acknowledge that evil is TRULY EVIL and not a part of God's plan for the Earth. Many spiritual people, especially from the New Age Movement, wrongly think that both good and evil must exist on Earth to maintain the balance of life. This attitude is escapism and evasion of responsibility and is one of the reasons that evil has remained active in our world. God's plan does not include sexual abuse of children, inhumane treatment of animals, human trafficking and glaring inequalities of income, to name a few. It is not a part of God's plan to see humans wearing masks for most of the day to protect themselves from the poisoned air—this is unnatural living that might become normal in future. Humans, to a great extent, have become insensitive to the evil around us and our 'spiritual' acceptance of evil is mainly responsible for it.

The fallen beings love nothing more than dragging people into a dualistic battle to fight evil. When you fight any evil with anger and violence, you only feed it more dark energy and strengthen it—the fight against it continues. Besides the discarnates on our planet, there are dark beings in the emotional realm who absorb the discordant energies released by humans. These dark beings use the accumulated energy to perpetuate evil in the physical realm. In a nutshell, you cannot put out a fire by adding more fire to it! The fight between Jews and Arabs has continued for decades now with no resolution in sight; the fight against terrorism, drugs, human trafficking, corruption and animal cruelty continues unabated—the victories won are short-lived. Evil does not disappear but keeps manifesting in new ways by changing forms. The world is full of well-intentioned crusaders against corruption and other evils; many of them have earned awards and citations for their work. But you see, this is how the fallen beings trick people into unwittingly furthering their diabolical agenda. They will let you win temporary victories and even ensure that you get fame and recognition for your so-called fight against evil. All this is a ploy to keep you trapped in a never-ending spiral of good versus evil fight; this has been happening for a long, long time.

Albert Einstein had said that one could never solve a problem from the same level of consciousness that created the problem. He was correct; however, this message has yet to sink in the minds of most people. You might have come across a situation where two people try to resolve a conflict and somehow arrive at a compromise. But the issue is not resolved—there is still anger simmering inside. Neither of them has looked at the issue from a broader perspective. If even one of them transcends the earlier level of consciousness, they can perhaps show the other person a higher perspective. If the latter agrees, they both can arrive at a permanent solution to the issue. Even in global issues such as the Arab and Jew conflict, the parties involved continue to feed the energy of anger, hatred and suspicion to the conflict—the beast becomes stronger and ensures no solution is found that resolves the conflict permanently. The learning here is that if you try to solve a problem or a conflict from the same state of mind that created it, you will get a temporary solution or no solution; the issue will remain simmering in the background waiting to explode any minute. The solution will be much better if we resolve the conflict from a state of consciousness more expansive than the one that created the discord. Much to the chagrin of the fallen beings, most of the world's population has transcended the consciousness of world wars, so this is why the third world war has not taken place till now and hopefully never does!

The key to defeating the evil in this world is that humankind must raise its consciousness. As more people expand their consciousness, more spiritual light from all their I-AM-Presences will flood the Earth. As a result, the Earth's vibration and frequency will increase, making it progressively difficult for the low-vibration fallen beings to adapt to the changing planet.

This phenomenon is similar to several ancient species disappearing because they could not acclimatize to the changing Earth. The raised frequency of our planet will push the fallen ones out of embodiment. They will never again re-embody on Earth, and this is how evil in our world will end forever.

The fallen beings constitute only about 2% of the world's population, but they have enormous power, money and resources at their disposal. They have infected humankind with the fallen consciousness. Often, many ethical and moral people including activists and anti-corruption crusaders, succumb to the fallen consciousness and become corrupt minions of the fallen ones. When the frequency and energy of our planet rises, it will affect such people, and they will realise their follies and blunders. Many of them will turn against the evil forces and expose them. You need not be an activist against corruption or a law officer. You can be from any walk of life and work towards eradicating evil by raising your consciousness. If you are an activist, you can continue your job but work also towards raising your consciousness so that you act from the inner peace of your Conscious-Self and not your reactionary Unconscious-Self. You need not react with anger and hatred, as this will energise the very evil you are fighting. Your dark energies will pollute your four lower bodies and contribute towards disturbing the Earth's energy field.

Currently, there are millions of people who can significantly raise their current level of consciousness; out of these millions there are 10000 people who have the potential to manifest full Christhood. You can scarcely imagine the changes that will happen on Earth if a critical mass of these people strives to attain Christhood—much evil will vanish.

CHAPTER 22
Our Ascended Teachers

The ascended masters are world teachers who guide humanity in accordance with the divine plan. They are called ascended beings because they have merged with their I-AM-Presence and are totally out of the vibrational atmosphere of the Earth; therefore, they are perfect and infallible. Many ascended masters were once human and lived on Earth just like us. They too faced life's challenges, tribulations, failures and disappointments, but by their own efforts achieved mastery over the Earth's discordant energies. They expanded their consciousness to an extent where they freed themselves from the cycle of birth and death and ascended to the higher realms.

Many of these masters were once prophets and great spiritual teachers on Earth. Three notable examples are Krishna, Buddha and Jesus. All spiritual teachings have been brought to Earth, directly or indirectly, by the ascended masters. Unfortunately, the teachings get distorted and crystallise into orthodox religions and doctrines that only enslave people instead of freeing them. The ascended masters have boundless love and compassion for humankind and joyfully seek to assist humanity in its spiritual evolution. They are the great watchers of humankind and know everything that is happening on Earth. They know that organised religions have failed miserably in bringing peace and happiness in our world. Therefore, they are bringing their teachings to humankind through various messengers; this is critically needed today or else humankind will destroy itself. The ascended masters are now revealing knowledge about the I-AM-Presence, Christ-Self, causal body, four lower bodies, threefold unfed flame, seven rays and much more, to the masses. In earlier ages, this knowledge was imparted to students in secret spiritual retreats.

Some of the ascended masters who are currently working for planet Earth are Lord Maitreya, Master Chananda, Buddha, Serapis Bey, Krishna, Saint Germain, Jesus Christ, Master More*, Lady Nada, Master Kuthumi, Master Lanto and Mother Mary. They are collectively known as the 'Ascended Council of Light' and also 'The Great White Brotherhood'. Humanity should feel immensely grateful to this team of ascended beings that is working to take the Earth into the next Golden Age. Many ascended masters can easily shift to higher spheres, but out of compassion for humankind they have decided to stay in the etheric realms of our current sphere. They guide humanity's evolution from the higher etheric realms. The masters desire that we see them as our elder brothers and sisters who have moved into the light ahead of us and now want to help us join them in the ascended realms.

It is of vital importance to realise that no ascended master is a Hindu, Christian, Muslim, Indian, American and so on. Religions, doctrines and political boundaries are man-made constructs and apply only to the Earth realm and not the higher vibrational realms where the masters reside. The teachings of every master are universal and cannot be boxed into a religion. Krishna, Jesus and Buddha should not be seen as Hindu, Christian and Buddhist Gods, despite what orthodox religions and scriptures say. The ascended masters have a very high level of consciousness; they have an immensely expansive view of life on Earth. As you expand your consciousness, you too will experience your religion losing its grip on you, and you becoming a universal being. The ascended masters are aligned to the will of the Creator God who is far beyond what orthodox religions portray Him.

Humanity has evolved in the last two and a half thousand years and our planet has moved from the Piscean Age to the Aquarian Age (inaugurated by the masters in March 2010). Therefore, the ascended masters felt it necessary to release new teachings and techniques through their messengers. As humankind evolves, even spiritual teachings need to be upgraded just as the academic syllabus changes with grades; the teachings in organised religions are frozen. These ascended masters' teachings are for the new age and some parts of the teachings are sure to shake your established belief patterns. You should approach the teachings with an open mind that is unprejudiced by your existing religious beliefs. Truth is beyond all organised religions, dogmas, doctrines and theology. In my opinion, the most beautiful thing about the ascended master teachings is that they teach us that every human being is a potential ascended master. Prophets such as Jesus demonstrated that they were not ready-made and extra-special beings created by a partial God; therefore, every spiritual seeker could follow their example. Unfortunately, organised religions turned the prophets into idols of worship with such supernaturally high positions that it became impossible for most people to relate to them personally.

The cosmic law forbids the ascended masters from interfering with the free will of humans, so they never promise to do any work on our behalf. What they expect from us is this:

- Study their teachings and work sincerely towards raising our consciousness. The masters neither desire to be worshipped nor encourage worshipping God. The Creator only desires His children to realise their true identity and join Him. The practice of mechanical ritualistic worship in orthodox religions is encouraged by fallen beings to keep humanity enslaved.

- Be a reference point for others but never try to convert them to these teachings through force or manipulation as it is the greatest sin to violate someone else's free will.

- Work towards changing the world or give any service to society, but only through the state of inner peace that one attains when their consciousness has sufficiently expanded. Using violence and aggression, and getting caught in dualistic battles to resolve issues is not the ascended master's way.

The ascended masters desire to release in our world several advanced technologies, such as free energy and ultra-fast zero-pollution travel. However, humankind needs to raise its consciousness so as not to misuse the new technologies and inventions. If the energies of our planet become purer, the masters will be able to communicate better with humanity. Another thing worth mentioning is that the masters want most people, after death, to enter the etheric realms. The masters have their spiritual retreats in the etheric realms where spiritual training is provided to lifestreams for their further evolution. Currently, most people after death enter the emotional realm; some enter the mental realm and few enter the etheric realms. You can enter the etheric retreats of the masters only if you have spiritually evolved to some extent during your embodiment on Earth. Every human being, no matter how evil, after death, sees a brilliant light that leads to the etheric realms. Nevertheless, lifestreams with low consciousness cannot enter the light. They get stuck in the emotional or mental realms—this is obviously not what the masters want. Those lifestreams that have lived depraved lives in their earthly embodiments enter the lower sub-realms of the emotional realm. These sub-realms are astral hells, and the lifestreams there undergo severe agony and suffering for their vicious deeds in their earthly life.

You might be curious as to why there is no mention of the ascended masters in the various religions of the world. It is so because the fallen beings corrupted every religion (I repeat, every) and also took credit for themselves for whatever the masses thought to be right in religions. We do, however, find traces of mention in several sacred texts of various religions that in earlier times humankind used to talk to 'Gods' and 'angelic beings'. These Gods and angelic beings were the masters who were then visible to human beings because the energies of the Earth were then purer. After the Fall of Man, the Earth's energies became dense, so the ascended masters are no longer visible to ordinary human sight.

The Messengers

The ascended masters select the messengers. Some qualities that a messenger should possess are an unselfish nature and a desire to help humanity awaken spiritually. Some of the current messengers are Kim Michaels and Peter Mt. Shasta. The earlier messengers included Guy Ballard (Saint Germain Foundation), Geraldine Innocente (Bridge to Freedom) and Elizabeth Claire Prophet (Summit Lighthouse). The messengers take dictations from the ascended masters by attuning their consciousness with the latter. The ascended masters started their mission of assisting humanity in the year 1930 when Saint Germain started giving discourses to Guy Ballard and later also his wife Edna Ballard. Saint Germain is the Chohan of the violet flame, and it was he who brought knowledge of this sacred flame to humanity. After the Ballards, the ascended masters continued giving dictations to Geraldine Innocente, Elizabeth Claire Prophet, Peter Mt. Shasta, Kim Michaels and others. The dictations continue to this day, and the masters ensure that no one person or organisation has a monopoly on the teachings.

I have greatly benefitted from the books of Kim Michaels, Peter Mt. Shasta and Saint Germain Foundation. I recommend all books by Kim Michaels and Peter Mt. Shasta. Kim Michaels is an indefatigable messenger of the ascended masters. If you are new to his books, you should start with 'The Power of Self: A Practical Guide to Knowing the Self'. Another book by Kim Michaels that I recommend is "Healing Your Spiritual Traumas".

I was able to internalise the teachings of the ascended masters and was guided by my Christ-Self to write this book.

Besides the techniques stated in this book, other potent techniques are decrees and invocations which the ascended masters transmit to their messengers.

Kim's books have many powerful decrees for personal spiritual growth and changing the world. If *you use decrees and invocations, you will balance a lot of your karma and make quick spiritual progress. I <u>strongly recommend</u> giving decrees.*

How Decrees & Invocations Work

Decrees and invocations work on the principle of sound energy. We live in an ocean of energy. Just as ripples are created when a pebble is thrown into a pond, waves are created in the energy field around us when sound such as through human speech is generated. When you do decrees and invocations, the energy of your speech goes out to make beneficial changes in your life or the world. Decrees are much more powerful than prayers.

A Word of Caution

At one time, I doubted the existence of the ascended masters but a couple of incidents that are too personal to share convinced me otherwise—this happens to many people. The fallen beings have two big fears: humanity raising its consciousness and a critical mass of people attaining Christhood. The control that fallen beings exert on the world is inversely proportional to the level of consciousness of humankind. In every age, dark forces have attacked prophets, enlightened masters and the disciples. Several people viciously attacked Guy Ballard (during his active years as a messenger) and accused him of being a charlatan. Many messengers have faced such attacks. The sinister force works through vicious people who are often media persons, fanatic religious leaders, prejudiced and closed-minded rationalists. You might come across half baked, one-sided, partial and malicious information on the Internet or elsewhere about the masters and the messengers; do not give any credence to it but test the teachings and see it for yourself. The proof of the pudding is in the eating. The Earth has such dense energies that even the greatest of masters, when they embody on Earth, make mistakes. Going by this logic, even the messengers of the ascended masters are not perfect and have some human failings as all of us have. Perfection is not something static but an ongoing ever-evolving process.

Retreats of the Ascended Masters

Some of the retreats of the ascended masters are mentioned here. These retreats are in the etheric realm and many ascended master students travel to these retreats at night in their etheric bodies to receive spiritual instructions. They usually do not remember anything upon waking up, but the learning is stored in their etheric bodies and slowly but steadily refines their consciousness. Records and knowledge of all earlier civilisations and the authentic history of the Earth are kept in these retreats. In these retreats, the masters harness spiritual energies which they subsequently release to Earth.

- Master More*: He is the master of the first ray (electric blue) and the throat chakra. His retreat is located in Darjeeling, India.

- Lord Lanto: Master of the second ray (yellow) and the crown chakra. His retreat is in Grand Teton mountains in Wyoming USA.

- Paul, the Venetian: He is the lord of the third ray (pink) and the heart chakra. His retreat is, Château de Liberté, Southern France Temple of the Sun, New York.

- Serapis Bey: He is the master of the fourth ray (pure white) and base chakra. His retreat is based out of Luxor, Egypt.

- Hilarion: He is the lord of the fifth ray (green) and the third-eye chakra. His retreat is in Crete, Greece.

- Lady Nada: She is the master of the sixth ray (purple and gold) and the solar plexus chakra. Her retreat is in Saudi Arabia.

- Saint Germain: He is the lord of the seventh ray (violet) and the soul chakra. His retreats are in Transylvania, Romania and also in Table Mountain, Wyoming, USA.

There are many more retreats of other ascended teachers in the etheric realms. A great book to know about the retreats is 'The Masters and their Retreats" by Elizabeth Claire Prophet.

____

* Master More is also known as El Morya or Al Morya.

CHAPTER 23
Teacher and Student

A true spiritual master is a rare phenomenon and you can consider yourself truly fortunate if you have found one. A real spiritual teacher must be significantly above the 48th level of consciousness. Every spiritual teacher is not a master because spiritual mastery means 'mind over matter', and this is achieved only after crossing the 96th level of consciousness. The concept 'mind over matter' means having the ability to manipulate the vibratory rate of electrons present in all matter—this is how prophets such as Krishna and Jesus performed miracles. Upon attaining higher levels of consciousness, one can gain mastery over matter—this means commanding obedience from the four elements (fire, earth, water, air). Therefore, there is nothing really miraculous about miracles; it is a higher science that cannot be understood through ordinary consciousness.

You must not think that only a master can be your spiritual teacher. Even a spiritual teacher who is below the level of mastery can be a spiritual teacher. Prophets arrive with missions deservedly assigned to them by their preceptors in the higher realms. Not all spiritual teachers attain the spiritual heights of prophets, such as Krishna and Jesus, but that does not mean that they cannot be good teachers.

Every spiritual student should know that there is no such thing as the ultimate spiritual teaching. The Creator releases its sparks in the form of beings who journey through different spheres, learn from their experiences and rejoin the Creator. A being can develop the full consciousness of the Creator God and become a Creator itself—growth in consciousness has no end because consciousness is infinite. Therefore, no spiritual master will ever claim that their teachings are definitive and that there can be no higher truths. Likewise, no spiritual seeker should ever search for the ultimate teaching. Every seeker should internalise what is taught by their spiritual teacher, transcend those teachings and seek higher teachings. Organised religions attract a lot of followers because they do not encourage transcendence of consciousness. It suits organised religions perfectly if the followers remain the same people year after year and satisfy themselves only with outer rituals. Orthodox religions have made people spiritually lackadaisical and lazy.

Qualities of an Authentic Spiritual Teacher

The more the following qualities a spiritual teacher displays, the closer they are to the 144th level of consciousness. *Please note that in this section, I am referring only to spiritual teachers. Individuals such as scholars, priests, preachers, religious teachers and theologians mostly have bookish knowledge of scriptures and religious texts. Such people have no spiritual attainment and are at ordinary levels of consciousness, very often below the 48th.*

- **Above religion** - A genuine spiritual teacher is above all organised religions, so never propagates any, including the one they belong to by birth. They are only interested in the spiritual growth of their students; consequently, their teachings and techniques aim only at expanding the consciousness of their students. The teachings of a spiritual teacher guide students to rise above the divisions of religions, castes, sects, doctrines and dogmas. A real teacher will not condemn any religion but will make you realise that the outer path of organised religion is right only up to a certain point.

- **Authentic** - There is a misconception that a spiritual person is always polite, warm and pleasant. A spiritual teacher is an authentic person and will get angry when the occasion demands it. They do not react but act as the situation demands it—Jesus's turning the tables of the greedy moneylenders at the temple in Jerusalem is an example. Indeed, some Zen masters physically hit their students to discipline them. Nonetheless, the anger of a genuine spiritual teacher is total and motivated solely by the desire to correct the student. It comes from their Conscious-Self and does not leave any scar in their four lower bodies. A real teacher, for a genuine reason, can display rudeness or indifference towards a student.

- **Above greed** - No sincere spiritual teacher is greedy to attract followers—they never encourage their students to manipulate others into becoming students or followers. Cult worship, numbers game and possessiveness of students are not something a good teacher seeks and displays. A good teacher, if they feel the student's lessons with them are complete, will gladly set the student free. They will encourage the student to find another teacher who will help the latter with other aspects of spiritual growth. Such a teacher is also beyond greed for money and material possessions. However, it is all right if a sincere spiritual teacher is running an organisation that charges reasonably for books, etc. A spiritual teacher also needs a livelihood and God does not drop money from heaven. Watch out, if your teacher revels in luxuries and comforts while their followers live a difficult life.

- **Fearless** - Prophets and masters never sugar-coat their words to dilute the truth. The fearlessness of Jesus and Buddha made many people uncomfortable, especially benighted priests and officials. A genuine spiritual teacher will not hesitate to speak out and expose the ills in religions: superstitions, useless rituals, fanaticism and caste system, to name a few. They are nonconformists and do not massage anyone's ego, no matter how important that person is. A spiritual master is a rebel but with a cause. It is a teacher's sacred duty to demolish the false beliefs of their students; therefore, they need to be fearless.

- **Humility** - Humility is one of the essential traits of a real spiritual teacher. Genuine teachers are free from spiritual pride and never take the devotion and love of their students for granted. There is a saying that the heavier a tree is with fruits, the more it will bend. An authentic spiritual teacher is like this tree—their humility is directly proportional to their spiritual insight and wisdom. Please be aware that negative energies on Earth are so dense that they cause even enlightened masters to sometimes make mistakes. A genuine teacher will not try to defend their mistakes but will humbly accept them and move on.

- **Transcend** - Every spiritual teacher is also a student and a seeker; they cannot become complacent with their spiritual attainment. A good teacher must keep on learning to stay relevant; this is applicable not just to academics but also spirituality. The more spiritually evolved the teacher is, the more they speak from their own experiences and quote less from the scriptures. Every authentic spiritual teacher must aim to become a spiritual master. It is not just on Earth but also in the higher realms and spheres that ascended beings are constantly evolving.

- **Articulate** - An effective spiritual teacher must explain spiritual concepts in simple language and preferably give examples from real-life experiences. By using difficult words, a spiritual teacher may confuse or intimidate their students. Articulation also includes explaining a concept from different angles to give a comprehensive understanding to the student. A true spiritual teacher will refrain from using too much of difficult spiritual jargon from the scriptures and adapt their teachings to suit the modern age. In ancient days, the priesthood used to hide mystical knowledge from the masses by coding them in languages unknown to most people; this cannot be the practice in the current age.

Spiritual Path versus Self-Help

I have great respect for self-help teachers; they have done lots to improve life. However, there is a difference between the spiritual path and the self-help path. The latter is the outer path and is primarily concerned with the Unconscious-Self. A self-help teacher may make you give up smoking—the Self within you that loves to smoke becomes quiet but is awake. So you have worked on yourself but at the mental level. The habit can relapse or in its place some other wrong habit may crop up. The human mind has a mind of its own and it is often vindictive when forced to do something. In the path of Christ Consciousness, your expanding consciousness will refine your senses so much that smoking will drop automatically—the Self within you that loves to smoke dissolves!

The self-help path deals with manipulating the Selves, but the path to Christhood involves dissolving the Selves. A self-help teacher works on refining your personality while a spiritual teacher works on transforming your consciousness.

For Genuine Spiritual Seekers

- There are many aspects to consciousness and often one teacher or path is unable to deal with all them. If you feel your lessons with a teacher are complete, and they cannot help you further, you should seek another teacher or path. A sincere spiritual seeker does not get stuck to any teacher, guru or organisation. Your spiritual growth is too precious to be pawned to any misguided sense of loyalty to a teacher, path or organisation. However, if you move before completing your lessons and keep jumping from one teacher to another, you will become a spiritual tourist and ultimately learn nothing. Observe yourself without prejudice, and you will know when your growth under a teacher has stopped—this is something only you can tell.

- There is a lot of popcorn spirituality out there in the market and many false gurus and teachers claim to give instant enlightenment. It would be best to avoid such people like the plague. Spiritual growth is a gradual process and there is no such thing as instant enlightenment. Many false teachers may tempt you to take specific drugs and upon using them, you may experience a false and temporary sense of expansion of consciousness. Nevertheless, this is very dangerous and can lead to a sudden loss of identity for which you are not prepared; this can lead to insanity or mental illness. If you want to expand your consciousness, there are no shortcuts.

- Do not treat your spiritual teacher as a self-help guru or life-coach. Your teacher's primary goal is to help you expand your consciousness and not advise you on your career and personal relationships. At times they can give some suggestions; however, do not make it a habit to annoy them on these matters. As your consciousness expands, you will start getting the right guidance from your Christ-Self.

- Do not thrust your projections and expectations upon your spiritual teacher. Many spiritual students have a pre-built image of how a spiritual teacher should behave. If the teacher does not fit into their image, they denounce the teacher as a fake teacher or a fraud. If your spiritual teacher is genuine, he/she will not care to fit into your image but will be an authentic individual.

- Very often, when a spiritual organisation becomes popular, the dark forces send their agents and representatives to join the organisation and destroy it. These minions work from within the organisation to tarnish its image. Many genuine teachers have had false and exaggerated allegations levelled against them that have damaged their reputation. As a spiritual student, do not be gullible and believe everything, but keep your eyes open to your surroundings. Be aware, however, that there are many false teachers in the spiritual market, so use your discrimination and intuition in selecting a preceptor.

- Please remember that a teacher with a vast number of disciples may be a genuine teacher but may still not be right for you. Usually, such teachers cater to middle-level students who are not ready to rise beyond a certain level of consciousness. Nevertheless, nothing definitive can be said about this as such a teacher may sometimes give advanced teachings—it is best to use your discrimination. If you think you have reached an advanced stage, you would probably need a teacher with a limited following of advanced students. The key point is not to choose a teacher only because of their disciple count. Also, beware of false prophets who are often charismatic and excellent communicators. You must not get impressed by their large following because such a false teacher only seeks to manipulate and exploit.

- No spiritual seeker should think that pursuing the spiritual path means neglecting one's worldly life. It is absolutely wrong to equate spirituality with lack, poverty and failure. The I-AM-Presence of an individual always seeks abundance for its human. This abundance means not only increased finances but also better health, relationships and more mental freedom. In the present age, it is not advisable to seek solitude in the mountains to meditate, but one must live in the world and fulfil their material and spiritual obligations. There is absolutely nothing wrong if a spiritual aspirant earns lots of money ethically and by adding value to society. Be very cautious of teachers who advise you to renounce the world. Becoming a monk or nun is a tradition in some orthodox religions but does not guarantee spiritual growth—many renunciants are at ordinary levels of consciousness.

Spiritual Experiences

Spiritual experiences should not be discussed with others as it has many pitfalls and can retard your progress indefinitely. Here are some important reasons why you should never discuss your spiritual growth with others. Please take note that here I am discussing spiritual experiences that an aspirant undergoes and not the practice of spirituality. It may not be possible (and perhaps also not necessary) to hide your spiritual practices from your family members. As you progress on the spiritual path, and as your consciousness expands, you will notice beneficial changes in your nature and also your life. At an advanced stage you might even have mystical experiences—it is these changes and experiences that I am referring to in this chapter. Let us now examine why you should not discuss these with others.

- It may incite jealousy in others, and this could even include family members and other loved ones. The reason is that deep inside, every person who lives an unconscious life, knows that they are missing something. Their worldly life and material success do not give them the wholeness they inwardly crave. Therefore, at a deeper level, they seek wholeness, not realising that it can be attained only by following the path of Christhood. However, their ego, acting through the Unconscious-Self, keeps them away from seeking anything higher. Consequently, they often become jealous when they see another person walking the path of real self-actualisation. Also, unlike as in material life where every human being is expendable, your spiritual growth is something that in the whole world only you can do. Nobody, not even the ascended masters, can do it on your behalf. When you embark on the path of self-actualisation, you are doing something unique, so this often incites envy in others.

- Discussing your progress with others may inflate your ego, especially if you are very articulate and impress others with details of the path or techniques you follow. People may misperceive you as someone who likes to boast and portray themselves as superior to others. Spiritual ego is downright poisonous and dangerous because it enters through the back door. Many spiritual students stop making progress because they start bragging about their spiritual achievements.

- The more you discuss your spiritual progress with others, the wider the portal you open for other people's opinions to interfere with your progress. People with materialistic tendencies may scoff at you or make sarcastic remarks in the garb of jest to discourage you. Some spiritual students may try persuading you that their path is superior to yours, so you should switch over. Be aware that, in the preliminary stages, most spiritual aspirants are not very confident of their own chosen paths; by converting others, they get a false assurance that they have chosen the correct teacher or organisation for themselves. Unless your mind is sturdy, you are always open to going astray because of the suggestions of other people. A person entrenched in organised religion, rituals, dogmas and doctrines knows little or nothing about consciousness and is unlikely to comprehend the inner path. If you discuss your spiritual practices with such people, it may provoke arguments, heated exchanges and bickering—this will needlessly disturb you. The other person's religious inclinations or spiritual growth are none of your business! Only when you reach a certain level of Christhood that you should, if you get an opportunity, get into debates or discussions and challenge the views of others. However, this should be done not to force them to change or prove you are superior to them. It should show them a higher perspective and leaving it to them whether they accept it or not.

- With your growth in Christ Consciousness, your I-AM-Presence will reveal more to you. You might have experiences such as visions and prophetic dreams. These experiences are sacred and deeply personal, and if you discuss them with others, you are likely to stop having them. Please do not make them a topic of discussion to entertain others. In the worst scenario, people may even challenge you to prove the veracity of your experiences.

To sum it up, the spiritual path is challenging but infinitely rewarding. Your journey concerns you alone, so you should discuss your spiritual experiences only with your teacher or preceptor and no one else. But remember that your ultimate teacher is your Christ-Self.

CHAPTER 24
Recapitulation

I thought it best to recapitulate the salient points in this book.

- In the beginning, there was only the Creator God, there was no form, and only pure spirit and darkness existed; the Creator felt lonely.

- Out of His own light known as the Universal-Light-Substance, the Creator created seven spheres in succession.

- The spheres were created in a way that the beings in it would not remember that they were a part of the Creator. With every successive sphere the forgetfulness of the beings increases—this is the basis for the drama of all Creation.

- The beings in the sphere would create, learn, evolve, and remember their connection with the Creator. These beings would then ascend and join the Creator in the spiritual realms.

- The first six spheres have ascended. The seventh sphere comprises the material universe and is yet to ascend. Currently, there is not enough spiritual light in the seventh sphere so it is unascended; the Creator expects the beings in this sphere to draw light from their higher selves.

- The Earth resides in the material universe. The material universe has four realms, etheric, mental, emotional and physical. Earth is in the physical plane.

- The energies of the Earth are dense and vibrate at a lower rate than the energies of the other realms and higher spheres.

****

- Evil on Earth originated because of the fallen beings that descended from earlier spheres. They polluted the consciousness of humans and this lead to the Fall of Man.

- The fallen ones do not want humankind to learn of higher realities and the real Creator. They want to control humanity by keeping it in spiritual darkness.

- The sinister force originated because of the fallen beings. It gets energy and sustenance from the impure thoughts of humankind, including fallen beings. Discarnates also strengthen the sinister force in many ways.

- Vicious thoughts of humankind adversely affect Nature, causing it to rebel in the form of natural disasters, such as earthquakes and floods.

- Evil can be defeated permanently only if a critical mass of humankind raise their consciousness. When consciousness is raised, more spiritual light from the higher realms enters into the atmosphere of Earth and eradicates the darkness of evil.

****

- The I-AM-Presence of every person is the individualised presence of God that wants to bring beauty and harmony in the individual's life and also assist in creating a beautiful Earth.

- The I-AM-Presence experiences life in the physical realm through a part of itself known as the Conscious-Self. However, it gives free will to the Conscious-Self and does not interfere unless invoked.

- The Conscious-Self forgets its connection to its I-AM-Presence because of the dense energies on Earth and impurities in the four lower bodies. It creates the ego as a self-defence mechanism; the ego creates the Selves that collectively form the Unconscious-Self.

- At some point, the Unconscious-Self takes over entirely, and the Conscious-Self recedes into the background. The Unconscious-Self driven by the ego now runs the individual's life. The personality created by the Unconscious-Self reflects the fears and insecurities of the ego.

- Living through the Unconscious-Self results in tribulations, such as diseases, ailments, accidents and misfortunes—it is the hard way to live.

- The Conscious-Self should reclaim its true identity (its I-AM-Presence)—this is also known as ascension. For this it is imperative to dissolve the Unconscious-Self; this is done by purifying one's four lower bodies. Unless the four lower bodies are purified, it is impossible to make spiritual progress no matter what religions and scriptures say.

- When ascension happens, one need not ever embody again on a dark planet, such as the Earth. One shifts either to more evolved planets in the seventh sphere or the sixth sphere.

- When a person evolves spiritually they exert an upward pull on the collective consciousness of all people on Earth.

- Humankind must recognise sound psychological health and mental freedom instead of wealth and material success as true abundance.

- Mental freedom means freedom from toxic emotions; need to seek validation and praise from others; doctrines, dogmas, theories and concepts; religious, racial and caste bias; etc.

- Only spiritual growth can bring mental freedom. If humanity shifts its focus towards attaining psychological well-being, the trajectory of human evolution will change course towards the next Golden Age.

****

- Those who attain ascension are known as ascended masters or ascended beings.

- A group of ascended masters who dwell in the etheric realm are actively working for the evolution of the people on Earth.

- Ascended masters brought to humankind knowledge of I-AM-Presence, unfed flame, violet flame and much more.

- The ascended masters are looking to awaken a critical mass of human beings who by raising their consciousness can bring remarkable changes to our planet.

The world needs scientists, engineers, researchers and more. However, what it needs most are Christed beings who draw spiritual light from their I-AM-Presences and spread this light all over the planet. Your life's report card should show a significant expansion in your consciousness from youth to old age—this is the highest and the only truly worthwhile success in life.

About The Author

 Manish Jaitly is an avid spiritual seeker and has been into spirituality for many years now. Since his childhood, he has intuitively felt that there was more to life than what is visible to our senses. After internalising the teachings of several masters, he felt guided to write this book. One cannot go on taking from the world and, after a stage, has to start sharing too. This is Manish's first book, and he hopes to write many more (non-fiction and fiction). He feels he has many stories to tell.

Manish is an analytics professional and a passionate dog lover.

Manish's websites:

MJAITLY.COM

DOGWARD.COM

He can be contacted at:

info@mjaitly.com